A Nautical Novice

(Or A FLY on the BOAT)

By

Michael K Chapman

A Nautical Novice

Tales of fun and humorous anecdotes based on a life on the water in sailing boats and motor boats. From a totally inexperienced sailor to a complete moron on the water, read how life changes when caught by that mysterious and very expensive malady known as, 'Messin about on the water' but less commonly termed Maritime Madness or Bungling Boater.

A Nautical Novice
(Or A FLY on the BOAT)

Dedicated to my greatly missed old friend, Peter.

Other titles by this Author.

A Fly on the Ward.

A Fly on the Garden Wall.

Non-fiction:

Humanology

Table of Contents.

Chapter One: Baptism.

My first dip into the world of boating, sailing and all things wet came quite unexpectedly. Up until the fateful day I had given no thought to the hobby of sailing, water did not hold any fascination for me. Perhaps because I swim like a brick, straight to the bottom, or because I like many others had sat chilled through the first showing of Jaws, a now infamous film about a killer shark. Of course my mind told me there were no Great White sharks off the coast where I lived, however my heart and my own brand of cowardness ruled that I stay as far away from water as humanly possible. Unless a bar of soap was required of course. But my opinions were soon to change, my swimming ability did not change or my conviction that I would soon be shark bait, but my interest in boats changed, and solely due to an unexpected turn of events.

I was working as a landscape gardener in my own firm and the business was doing well, it could be said that I was raking it in. I had many customers at that time, the majority of them were elderly and I was grateful for them. Most of my more mature customers required a maintenance service; my team and I would visit on a fortnightly basis usually and undertake all those jobs that my customers found difficult or simply tiresome. Over the years I had met many customers and always enjoyed the wide variety of people I worked for, some strange, some grumpy and some were totally weird. One morning a phone call came in and I wondered what I would face this time. After receiving instructions for work from the new customer, I decided to check out the job that same morning. Off I set in my rickety old van, armed to the teeth with lawnmowers, forks and spades and all other forms of torturous horticultural implements. Arriving at the location I was not surprised to discover my new customers were another elderly couple, named Hogh. My services were required to do battle with a garden that had become too unruly for the old couple to managed, so it became the chore of my firm to tame the raging beast. Within days work was progressing normally and without any mishaps until one fateful morning some time later.

At nine o'clock my team and I arrived at the property ready to face another day of grass cutting, pruning, weeding and other such delights that accompany the modern garden. I swung open the newly hung gate and knocked on the front door to receive our orders for the day. Almost immediately the door opened and a tearful Mrs Hogh peered at me through red rimmed eyes. With uncanny insight I realised she may be upset. Thinking she had received bad news in the post or her husband had burnt the toast, I enquired into her state of health as solemnly as I could while striving to maintain my pleasant morning smile. I certainly did not expect her sobbed reply.

'I'm sorry,' she replied with a sniffle, 'you'll have to come back another day, my husband passed away last night and I cannot be thinking about the garden just yet.'

Well to say I was shocked would be an understatement, I simply stood and stared at her as my bewildered mind struggled to find the right words of sorrow and comfort that one needs to say in situations such as this. Instead all I managed was a feeble acknowledgment and a few muttered words offering our condolences. Leaving the poor woman to grieve we climbed aboard my old van and left to seek other employment for the day.

A week passed and I was trying to decide whether to call on Mrs Hogh and enquire how she was, when the phone rang. To my surprise a cheerful voice greeted me, the voice of Mrs Hogh. There was no trace of her loss as she requested that I call on her at the earliest opportunity to discuss the remaining work to be completed in her garden. I agreed and that evening I knocked uncertainly on her door, not knowing what to expect. Mrs Hogh asked me to enter and led me to a seat at her kitchen table. I was offered a cup of coffee and I accepted her offer. I took this little mistake quietly and drank the very weak *tea* while Mrs Hogh outlined her plan for the continuation of work on her property. Mrs Hogh sat opposite me at the table and while she chatted politely I studied her. She was a lady in or very near her eighth decade of life emphasised by her iron grey hair, small glasses perched upon her nose and the bright red lipstick battled to match her still red rimmed eyes. She was not tall, nor could she be termed fat, however I do recall I had the initial impression of a plump round dumpling that seldom ceased talking.

Mrs Hogh explained that with her husband's demise her finances were in a state of limbo. At that time she had no funds until her husband's pension was unlocked by the solicitors and the Will had been read and acted upon. As she spoke I had already decided to complete the work required and put my faith in Mrs

Hogh to settle her account as soon as her financial situation allowed. However she had other plans and these plans would lead me into a totally new and expensive but enjoyable lifestyle.

Mrs Hogh made me an offer I should have refused but considering her recent upset I instead eventually accepted. Mrs Hogh suggested I continue the work and in return she asked if I would take her husband's boat in lieu of payment. Well I was flabbergasted. In fact one could say I felt all at sea at her suggestion. A boat! What would I do with a boat? Admittedly I lived in an area very close to the sea but owning a boat had never crossed my mind. I would have been less surprised if she had offered me her ancient and wrinkly body in payment, but a boat, well that was another thing entirely. I stated I would consider her proposal and left in all reasonable haste.

I had been offered a boat once before and had quickly turned down the offer. My uncle had passed away some years before and my father had asked if I would like his boat. At that time I was in my late teens and beer and girls were my main interests, as is normal for a young male making his way deeper into sexual maturity. I had no idea what to do with a boat, where would I keep it? The back yard was hardly big enough for a twenty five foot Plymouth Pilot type vessel and how the heck would I get it in there, the garden path was only four foot wide. However I remembered the pleasant times spent on my uncle's boat when I was a young boy and he often took our family out for day trips out into the bay.

My recollections were of sunny days on a huge boat with my brother and sister beside me and my mother looking slightly apprehensive in the small cuddy. With the diesel engine thumping against the tide, a mackerel line over the stern where my brother hauled in fish by the bucket load, a grin on his face as the wind ruffled his hair. For myself I simply wanted to drive the thing. Whenever my uncle instructed me to steer back towards the harbour, I surreptitiously kept edging the boat back out to sea. I never wanted the trips to end. However as we grew older the boat trips declined, teenagers regularly fail to understand the basic pleasures in life and a day out on an old boat soon lost its appeal. Now years later here was my father offering me that same said vessel. I respectfully declined the offer from my father, and of course regretted it later when he sold it on for a paltry six thousand pounds! These days such boats sell for ten times as much. I can never admit to learning from my mistakes but when Mrs Hogh made the offer, I decided to give the matter serious consideration. I hoped I could make back my money by selling the craft at a later date, possibly I might even contemplate actually having a go in the thing - possibly. My mind was made up; I would take a look and base my decision on pure ignorance, and the dubious knowledge of a friend. I had an old friend who was very keen on boats and so I sought out his advice and guidance in the hope that I would avoid drowning myself.

I informed Mrs Hogh I would take a look at the boat before deciding, so that weekend I set off with my friend in tow and with wellies under my arm. Driving down to the moorings on a bright but cold Sunday morning, I had my first look at the lieu of payment I had been asked to accept. Of course I had no idea what the mud splattered wooden boat was, whether it would actually float or perhaps be offered up on a pile beneath a straw effigy of Guy Fawkes. Still bewildered at this odd turn of events, I pulled on my wellington boots and approached the sad looking boat - and promptly stuck fast into the mud on which the boat rested. My old friend was obviously more prepared for this than I as he strode quickly over the mud, his footfalls hardly sinking at all, I was still stuck.

'Don't hang around,' he called with a smile, 'it's best to move quickly over the mud before your feet get chance to sink.'

Great I thought, way too late to pass on that useful piece of advice now as I pulled, pushed and dragged my boots from the sticky grasp of the black mud. By now my friend was beside the boat, leaning over the free board and peering inside the cockpit with eyes agleam. Eventually I reached him and also took a closer look at the hulk with its paint peeling, seaweed strands, bird poo and all other forms of sea detritus that littered the interior of the craft. So what did I see? I saw a wooden boat about nineteen feet long standing on two thick legs I was later informed were bilge keels. A cabin sat just off the middle of the boat and I could just make out what looked to me like beds and a cooker. I mentioned this to my friend and received one word in reply.

'Bunks.'

What the hell, why did every thing need to have a different name? If it was flat, had a mattress of sorts and one was expected to sleep on it, it was a bed!

'Well I think it's a Caprice Mark Two, nineteen foot long if I'm not mistaken. It's a sailing boat or yacht to you. It looks in reasonable nick so you may have a good deal here. What do you think?' enquired my friend.

I stared at the object in question and took a closer examination of the wreck in front of me. It stood on its two keels some two foot off the mud. A dark blue hull contrasted with the seagull splattered white decks and pale blue anti-slip patches painted strategically where I assumed one would attempt to stand without falling overboard. The cabin rose above the cockpit before dropping in height about six inches and sloping down the fore deck, two small windows on each side provided light into the cabin. A varnished hatch slide back and two washboards had to be removed to gain access to the interior. High sides flowed back from the cabin area along the deck sections of the sides, giving one, or namely me, a false impression of security from thrashing waves. A tiny hatch was situated upon the lower cabin roof and allowed one to chuck the anchor overboard in rough seas from inside the cabin, or so my friend informed me. Though what the heck would anyone be doing out on this floating disaster in rough seas I could not imagine. A long aluminium mast lay horizontal on the top of the cabin and stretched the length of the boat. A mast that appeared way too long to me, I suffered vertigo just looking at it, Lord knows how I would cope when the damn thing was upright and in place. Finally a metal rail surrounded the bow of the vessel, this too was painted in a light blue but much of the paint had long peeled off. At the back of the boat, or stern as I understand now, a thick wooden transom held the rudder where a sturdy, the only sturdy thing on the boat as far as I could see, tiller leaned over the transom allowing one to steer the thing. A bench like seat attached to the transom provided a place to rest while remaining at the tiller.

My friend, called John in case you wanted to know, had more foresight than me and had come equipped with a three step ladder in order that we could gain access to the inside of the boat. We climbed carefully up and over the gunnels and side decks into the cockpit, leaving our wellies protruding like sentinels in the mud beside the ladder. John was moving around like a child in an unattended toy shop, a smile fixed firmly upon his lips. I did not move around at first, I was frightened I would fall straight through the floor and land in a heap in the mud under the boat. But with John's assurance that all was fine, I too began to explore the innards of this potential submarine. The cockpit itself was surrounded by varnished wooden seats that also served as storage compartments, one on each side that adjoined the transom seat. The transom seat was simply a bench and I could just see a rusting fuel tank and battery holder swimming in the bilge water beneath it. A wooden floor lay under my feet and various items of marine paraphernalia were strune about, waiting in eagerness to trip me up and send me flying over the side into the black sticky mud.

John had removed the two wash boards and pushed back the sliding hatch by now and I peered around him into the gloomy recesses of the cabin. I could make out the two bunks, one either side of a narrow walkway that led to cushioned triangle that covered the bow end of the cabin. Just inside the entrance on the right, or starboard if you want to be precise, stood a simple Belling cooker upon the surface of a small cupboard that hid the gas bottle that provided the fuel for cooking. Beside the cooker was a small stainless steel sink and a pump tap. To my left, or to port there was another small cupboard like structure that when opened, revealed a pump action sea valve toilet in desperate need of a bucket full of bleach. Progressing further into the interior, John lifted the bunk mattresses to check the further storage space beneath, each compartment was filled with ropes, shackles, fenders and a rusty tin containing well out of date distress flares. And more water of course. So what was it John had stated?

'. . It looks in reasonable nick so you may have a good deal here.'. . .

Good nick? Was he looking at a different boat to me? It looked a real wreck, a ship wreck in fact. It would take a massive amount of work to make it sea worthy and I still did not know a hand saw from a screwdriver. In fact the only time I could cut a straight line in a piece of wood was when I was trying to cut a circle. How the hell was I going to fix this? I would have to inform Mrs Hogh I could not accept her offer. I could find plenty of fire wood along the shoreline, I had no need of this particular lump of marine wastage. In the heat of the moment I colourfully described my impression of this Marie Celeste to my surprised friend and followed with what I thought should be done with the thing.

Climbing from the boat in disgust, I discovered my stocking feet were soaking wet from the water that lay slopping inside the boat. Yet another delightful feature of this wooden hen house I thought angrily. I suggested we head off to the nearby pub and discuss the Titanic junior and its possible worth to a land loving, carpentry inadequate, unwilling and completely inexperienced sailor like me. I will admit the pub itself was lovely, a fishing theme provided much of the décor and the customers were friendly and showed an interest in joining our discussion. It soon became evident that most considered my potential heap of marine ply to be a worthwhile vessel indeed. John of course was thoroughly delighted with the prospect of repairing and eventually sailing the thing, so finally I relented under pressure and agreed to take ownership of the sad floating wreck called Lundy Mist.

Still unsure and apprehensive concerning my decision, I agreed to Mrs Hogh's offer at my next visit to her property, and there began my adventures on river and sea which have continued till this very day.

Chapter Two: A boat returns to life.

Work soon began on the Lundy Mist and John made himself my unofficial partner in this new venture. He simply could not wait until the time came for us to begin the proper examination of the vessel and form a list of repairs. After a second or less of consideration, I decided to allow John to take the lead, it seemed wise as I still had no idea what was what and how to recognise what was not what it should be. Confused? Yeah well so was I!

The following Saturday John and I set off down to the river armed with a variety of tools and of course, wellies. It did not take John long to assess the condition of the boat and begin enthusing about the possibilities if we repaired that, or altered this and replaced that. Within an hour my brain was swimming with new words such as shackle, cleat, bilge, forestay, sloop and boom. John scampered around the deck investigating all forms of strange contraptions attached to the deck that he assured me were there for a purpose, I politely nodded at him while scratching my head in bewilderment. The few facts I did retain in my aching head were that the Lundy Mist was a sloop, a Bermuda sloop to be precise, with one mast which held the main sail along with another length of aluminium tube called a boom. To the front a smaller sail would be attached from the mast to a link or similar device on the bow. Two wires were attached to the sides of the mast and came down to be secured on each side of the cabin. Yes I realise I am not using the correct terminology for the sails and fixings, but let's remember that at that time I had absolutely no idea what each thing was or for what purpose it existed. To me all I knew were sails, at least I knew that bit; the ropes, wires, sliding tracks and other assorted things one tied a rope to were a mystery. Basically it was similar to describing the parts of a motor vehicle to a five year old child, I could see and touch these strange objects but their function in life totally escaped me. However I did begin to learn. Slowly and with the patience of a saint, John instructed me in all things related to the art of sailing and eventually some of the information began to penetrate my landlubber's brain.

My friend John was a lovely guy. He was in his late sixties I think but one would not know it as he leaped about the boat grasping saw and hammer. He was around six foot tall, slim but not thin with a thick head of silver grey hair that always appeared to be out of control. I had met John through a mutual friend and we soon discovered we shared similar passions. We both loved motorcycles and most things mechanical, electrical and basically anything we could pull apart and fiddle with. The fact that these items rarely worked again after we had reassembled them held no discouragement for us, we carried on regardless. Over the years I had known John, he often regaled me with stories about sailing in his younger days and it was partly his stories and experience in the watery world that swayed me into accepting the Lundy Mist. John, despite his age, was delighted with my latest acquisition, providing a running commentary of each and every item he encountered, no matter how small and seemingly insignificant. John was my best friend and I looked upon him as my second father. So I watched and listened as he slipped back through the years, rekindling his past love of sailing and all things nautical.

At last John ran out of breath and patience so we decided it was time to actually do some of the repairs he had spoken of. We set about repairing the hull and any other gaping holes we came across. With his wood craft skills and my wallet we soon had the hull water tight and painted. In truth there was only one real patch of rotten wood in the hull. A patch I myself found quite by accident and to the amusement of John and a couple who were walking their dog nearby. While John crawled and clambered inside the boat, I had been tasked with the responsibility of checking the hull from the outside, in the mud. John had decided as I had youth on my side, I was approximately half his age, I could do all the underneath examinations. Lovely!

Sinking to my knees and even further into the rather smelly black mud, I manoeuvred myself as far under the keel as I could. A difficult task made much more arduous by the slippery, squidgy, pongy and very wet surface I was attempting to crawl over. Luckily I did have the foresight to don a set of industrial waterproof jacket and trousers, along with my wellies of course. So I felt safe in my armour of bright yellow as I slid beneath the boat. Huh! The armour proved to have chinks in it, in moments the mud had managed to seep into my wellies, down my neck and worst of all, it gained access to my both my back and my backside.

There is little comfort in cold gritty mud entering one's underwear, believe me!

At last my inspection of the boat's undercarriage was complete and I widened my search to the sides of the hull. By now my bright yellow suit was the colour of the mud itself as I moved along the hull, accompanied by the sound of a squish as my boots sank into the mud and a plop as I pulled them out again with each step. I moved slowly along, gently tapping the sides with the handle of a screwdriver, not too hard but enough to distinguish between the sound of solid wood and rotten wood, or so I thought. Finding no evidence of rot in the marine plywood sides, I grasped the small step ladder, propped it against one side of the boat and resting it on the upper hull stepped upon the first rung. Mistake! With what can only be described as a dull wet thud, the top of the ladder simply fell through that section of the freeboard like a hot knife through butter. This caused the base of the ladder to slip backwards in the slimy mud and as we all know, every action has an equal and opposite reaction, as the ladder base slipped backwards so I fell forwards. My chin hit the gunnels with a crack and again a reaction occurred, my chin rebounded off the gunnels and my head shot backwards taking my surprised body with it. Splat! I landed flat on my back spread eagled in the exact same mud I had only recently climbed out of. In seconds I had mud in my hair, in my ears and even more down my trousers, I was not a happy bunny.

A quiet laugh floated down from above as John leaned over the boat and peered down at me and then at the hole in the side. 'So you've found a patch of rot then? Alright we'll start on that bit. As soon as you're finished lying around down there, that is. Oh and maybe have a bit of a wash off in the river before you splatter everything else in mud?' I refrained from answering at that point.

The hole through which the ladder top had fallen was roughly two foot square and I was unbelieving that I had missed it during my examination with the screwdriver, however John belayed my fears and assured me he could fix it. So after a splash around in the river water to remove most of the mud from my exterior, we set off to purchase some wood, fibre glass filler and battening. Considering the state of me, I first returned home for a shower, a change of clothes and a peel of laughter from my family.

Working most weekends saw the hole in the freeboard repaired and newly painted in fresh pale blue paint with new anti-slip coating on the deck, and finally a new coat of varnish on the rudder and tiller. The windows were cleaned and all internal fittings and fixtures were cleaned, painted, vanished or thrown overboard. The bilges were emptied, including any stray conger eel, giant squid or kraken that had chosen the Lundy Mist as a new home. Although I have only used a short section to describe the work we undertook, I will explain that restoring the sloop took several months. Working mainly at weekends due to the arduous chore of employment and earning a living getting in the way of my spare time and at the clemency of the elements as usual. Often a boat is described as a money bucket with a hole in the bottom, and the Lundy Mist was no exception. John frequently offered to purchase any items required but as he was giving his labour and experience free, I deemed it unfair to have him spend his pension on what my wife considered as my little toy. My wife does not like boats as will become evident.

Finally the time came to mount the mast and attach the rigging to the boat and it was at this stage that we hit a wall; neither John nor I had any idea how to go about this relatively essential task. Luckily we had both recently enrolled on an RYA, Royal Yachting Association course, mainly I admit for my benefit as my sailing experience still consisted of a toy boat in the bath. On the RYA course I eventually learned that a sheet was not actually a sail but a rope. Damn stupid name for a rope but that is the nautical term for it. Sheets are a generic name for all kinds of ropes and wires that adorn a sloop, individual names become even more confusing. Jib sheet; jib halyard and jib stay, main halyard, mainsheet, shrouds and forestays all proved to be a minefield for someone as nautically inadequate as myself.

Following the explanation of the rigging came – navigation! Blimey what a headache. With charts, dividers, compass and slide rule I felt I was back at school. My personal sense of direction is poor at the best of times; I can get myself lost travelling a route I have known for years. Also trying to remember all the maths I was supposed to have learned in school, but now with age those memories had begun to fade. How I would be expected to plot and achieve a course on water totally escaped me. However, John and I completed the course and both passed, much to my surprise. The instructor was a retired product of the Royal Navy and had been around boats his entire life. So at the end of the course as the class celebrated over a few drinks, the instructor offered to help us step the mast, and true to his word a few days later saw the instructor, John and myself struggling to erect the mast.

I had purchased a mooring out on the river, which in truth was part estuary, and subject to tidal flows so using a magnificent old Sea Gull outboard engine, a long pole and a lot of luck we manoeuvred the boat from its river side mooring and out onto the main section of the river come estuary. Under guidance from the RYA instructor, we managed to position the Lundy Mist and tie it up alongside the very small quay, situated in front of the small hamlet that bordered the river. By standing on top of the quay, we were able to gain access to the top of the mast without me having to shin up the damn thing and inevitably end up in the water. With the instructor directing our actions we attached the shrouds and the halyards without me becoming entangled, a feat in itself I thought. Soon all the rigging along with the mast and boom were in place and it was time to hoist the sails.

I was worried that if we raised the sails the old boat would try to take off into the wild blue yonder, however both John and the RYA instructor assured me this would not happen, unless we tightened the sail which was not going to happen.

'Was it?' they both questioned me sternly.

I kept my hands away from all cleats and sheets and remained on my best behaviour, besides I was too frightened I would do something stupid and sink the damn thing. At last all was secured and John and I took the Lundy Mist for its first sail in many years. The instructor wisely decided to watch from the safety of the quay. Hoisting only the mainsail, John took charge of the vessel and we gently and very slowly sailed out to my moorings in the centre of the river. It was only a matter of half a mile or so from the quay to the moorings, but to me it felt like I was sailing the ocean. With the sun beating down, a warm breeze filling the mainsail and seagulls screeching high above, I realised this was the life for me. I had momentarily forgotten all those cold and wet weekends spent trying to repair the boat on which I now stood. My epic voyage came to an end as we reached the orange buoy that marked my mooring. Then followed the fiasco of trying to pick up the mooring strop with a boat hook I had discovered hiding beneath one of the bunk cushions and found by my butt as I sat down. Eventually and not without the occasional choice word or three, I managed to hook the strop and John showed me how to secure it to the bow cleat. So at last the Lundy Mist was at rest on its permanent moorings, a feat achieved with some difficulties, mainly because I did not have any idea what I was supposed to do and John had to constantly shout out instructions that I barely understood.

Once the boat was securely tied to the buoy, John showed me how to use the rolling boom to bring down and fold the mainsail. A rolling boom I soon discovered actually turned, or rather it could be wound on a pivoting axle, allowing the mainsail to be wound around the boom as one would wrap toilet paper onto the toilet roll in its centre. John next showed me how to tie down all the sheets, as by then I knew the correct terminology, especially the jib and main halyards as these tend to flap about in the wind and bang against the aluminium mast with a sound like a bell. John explained it was polite to do this as the local residents did not wish to be disturbed on a windy night by the sound of halyards rattling against the mast all night.

31

Once finished and everything secured to John's satisfaction, I stood on the fore deck and waved furiously towards the shore. A friend had offered to carry us from the Lundy Mist as the tide was in and I had forgotten one important piece of equipment. I still needed a smaller boat usually called a 'tender' or dingy. This was vital as, personally speaking, I cannot walk on water and it was my firm belief that neither could John. So how were we to escape the Lundy Mist when it was floating on fifteen feet of water? At last my friend spotted us and began to row his boat over to collect us. Attempting to walk on water could wait I decided.

Back on land and joined by the instructor, the four of us stood and gazed across the water at the sight of the Lundy Mist floating serenely upon the calm water with the sun glittering off its windows and chrome fittings. A job well done I thought. A few moments passed before we began discussing the mornings events and what was next to be done. My friend immediately suggested I obtain a tender, John and the instructor agreed, what was the point of having a sloop on the water if I could not reach it. I agreed and closed the subject as there were many other comments all four of us wished to discuss. So as is normally the case when a group of men have something to mull over, we all headed of to the pub in order to partake of some mental stimulus.

A week or so later I was delighted to come across a small dingy that I considered would suit my purpose exactly. Made of plywood the poor thing was resting up against a hedge in a secluded section of the river bank. It had certainly seen better years but in my opinion, one lump of wood was much the same as another. It was a boat; I needed a small boat so I bought the thing. I know better now. The dingy was very small, about seven foot long, four foot wide with a blunt bow and a single plank along its centre served as a seat. Another shorter plank served as a stern seat and made up the total inboard furniture. Luckily I did not pay much as I think the owner just wanted shot of it and I came along with the word *mug* written right across my forehead. I rang John and he drove the two miles from his home to the river to inspect my latest purchase. Standing there in his wellies he stared at my new acquisition in horror until he noticed the delighted and somewhat idiotic smile on my face and relented.

'OK, it'll do for now but it'll need some fixing up. Hope you didn't pay too much for this punt?' he said while scratching his head in despair at my nautical gullibility.

'There's no need to be rude! Like you say, it'll do for now.'

'A punt I said! That's what we call small boats with a squared off bow and flat bottom.' John corrected me.

I choose not to admit I had only paid the price of a pint of beer for it, in fact I had bought it while in the pub, perhaps that might explain it, but I said nothing. I did not want to push John too far. Admittedly it would not win any prizes for its appearance, or its state of repair but it was mine and I was thrilled, stupid but thrilled. So we borrowed a boat trailer and transported the boat back to my home where I could work on it, with suitable instruction from John of course. I did not consider what my wife might say about having an old wooden boat in her carefully tended garden, but I soon found out.

Upon closer inspection of the boat I discovered it too had a hole in it, right on the bottom but by now I felt I was an old hand at repairing boats so I set about removing the rotten wood around the hole and cutting and shaping new wood to insert in the gap like John had done on Lundy Mist. Days later and I had still not managed to get one square piece of plywood to fit smugly inside the square hole that gapped in the bottom of the - punt. At last a solution raised its head in my brain and out came the fibre glass kit. I would fix this damn thing if it killed me, if I did not then it would most likely drown me but hey ho, here we go. I inserted the piece of wood that fitted best, meaning the piece that left the smallest gap around its edge and then smothered the whole section in several coats of fibre glass. By the time I had finished the repaired section was most certainly the strongest part of the boat, and that was saying something. A coat of paint followed and it was ready to go, least I thought it was and that was all that concerned me.

In due course I managed to get the little boat back down to the river and with the aid of borrowed oars I took the poor wee thing for a row about. All seemed fine so I decided to find a suitable outboard engine because, with aching arms I concluded rowing a boat was not my idea of a leisurely hobby, it was too much like hard work. Having an engine push me along seemed a much better idea. Some time after the little tender had survived its river trails, I managed to obtain two outboard motors very cheaply. One was so old I could not identify it under all the coats of paint applied by numerous previous owners, the other engine was a British Seagull. I repeat, I was totally inexperienced in all things nautical and still had much to learn and that is my excuse for buying an ancient British Seagull.

The beastie in question was a Silver Century if I remember correctly, the best of the Seagull range I was told, reliable I was told, and fast I was told. I think the word *mug* had appeared again on my forehead when I bought it. Anyway with glee I fitted a new spark plug, cleaned the carburettor, replaced the missing pull cord with a piece of thin rope, sanded off the rust and was ready to go. I informed John about the Seagull and its pending trial by water but he declined to accompany me on that occasion. I found another gullible friend to join me and we set off for the river after mixing the required oil and fuel to a guesstimated ratio. I think I mixed it to forty parts petrol to one part oil but could not be sure, it was somewhere near anyway. My friend and I attached the now gleaming Seagull to the transom of the little tender, no mean feat as I learned at that very moment what the difference was between a long shaft and a short shaft engine. The long shaft Seagull stood proud of the transom by a foot or more until we manoeuvred the dingy into deeper water, water deep enough to flow over the tops of my wellies and fill them to the brim. At last with the outboard engine screwed down by its clamps, we got on board, emptied our wellington boots over the side and headed away from the slipway with great expectations.

We did not get far. With a cough, a splutter and something that sounded very much like a fart, the Seagull stopped, its engine died, silence. There we were, adrift not ten feet from the slipway with a dead engine in a little punt, and a coach full of holidaymakers stood on the quay happily clicking away with their cameras. Luckily I had once been a boy scout, so I had come prepared and had brought a pair of newly acquired oars with me. So with me positioned on the central seat and my friend sat on the transom seat, we rowed the little boat and our red faces back to the slipway again. I left my friend holding a rope attached to the boat on the edge of the slipway while I dashed back to the car park to fetch the other engine. I had decided to bring it along to possibly play with it after a spin with the Seagull, I had no idea if it would start nor did I know the required petrol to oil mix. With mad abandon I filled its little fuel tank from the can I had mixed for the Seagull and carried it to the boat.

My thoughtful friend had in the meanwhile, repositioned the useless Seagull to one side and helped as I clamped the unknown little engine in its place on the centre of the transom. By now all the holiday makers and the coach driver and several locals were all lined up on the quay, all eager to witness the next instalment of idiots in a boat. Hah! They were disappointed as the little engine roared into life at the second pull. I was so surprised I nearly drove it straight into the quay wall before remembering to steer. Not only was the little engine purring away nicely, I had noticed it was of the short shaft type and fitted the boat perfectly. We stayed out on the river for an hour, just messing about on the water. But alas time flies when one is having fun and eventually we headed back towards the now empty quay and slipway, our trip a success. I would deal with the Seagull when I returned to my home, to my shed and to my big hammer!

As it turned out, there was little wrong with the Seagull that could not be fixed easily, like actually turning the fuel on! In my rush to get on the water I had forgotten to pull the small petrol valve to the open position so the engine had run out of fuel as soon as the carburettor chamber had emptied. My fault I admit now, I did not admit it then but I will own up to repeating this mistake frequently, right up to this day in fact. Some people take longer to learn than others, and it seems I take even longer. As for the little engine, I was so impressed I carted it around all the marine workshops in the area until one old guy identified it as possibly an early four horse power Sea Bee. It too received an overhaul with a new spark plug, air filter and a clean and it stayed with me as a backup for many years, right up until its drive shaft broke and I sent it off to the great scrap yard in the sky.

But at that time I had two old but usable outboard engines, one repaired sloop and one little punt, kept afloat by a gallon of fibre glass resin, and still no idea about sailing. Let's face it, I did not even own one of those funny little imitation captain's hat with the tiny anchor on the front, the type all wannabe sailors wear whenever they venture to the seaside on holiday. But to be honest, even I would not wear one of those; it would be like wearing a huge advertisement upon my head, proclaiming to the world that I was a pretend sailor. Anyway, my old woolly hat would suffice, I always did have a tendency to dress down rather than up, a fact the wife hates. Maybe that is why I do it?

As I was now the proud owner of a sloop and a small wooden tub, only fit for use as a flower pot, John and another experienced sailor friend called Don decided I needed a crash course in marine activities and so began my lessons. Did I mention I am a slow learner? Don, a short stocky man about ten years older than me, with short dark curly hair and a great barrel chest and a pipe permanently dangling from his mouth offered to take me out on his boat. I had no idea what make of boat it was but I will just describe it as a twenty seven foot long, very sleek modern sloop. Don had sailed around virtually every coast in the world in one form of boat or another. So I felt assured that he had the skills and experience to stop me doing anything daft. Don often took part in yacht racing and threatened to take me along as a crew member on day, once I had learned which sheet was which and how to duck when the boom came over during a tack. See? I was already getting the hang of the nautical terminology; I could even tie on my life jacket all by myself!

Lessons started with a tour around Don's boat, him pointing out things I should be aware of, me following in bewilderment. All was going well but then Don untied the mooring line, grabbed the mainsheet, hoisted the mainsail and jib and off we shot. I was taken totally unaware by his actions. I had no idea he actually intended sailing that day, I thought I was only there for a tour of his boat. I did not expect to see it in action. Don's boat was kept on deep water mooring a half mile or so further down river from my drying mooring. I still foolishly thought the sea was too far away and that we would simply potter about on the river. No. As we sailed along serenely in the still waters of the river, it was calm that day but I did know that these same waters could become truly unrelenting in bad weather, or when we had the wind over tide occurrence. That is when the tide is flowing one way but the wind is blowing in the opposite direction. On that particular day there was hardly any wind and the water was mirror like, flat and unthreatening. Don kept me busy as he showed me how to steer the tiller, position the mainsail to catch the optimum wind and what each of the gadgets that the main sheet went through actually did. I admit by now I was enjoying myself greatly and took little notice of the landscape around me; my concentration was fixed firmly on what Don was attempting to drum into my empty head.

Finally Don pointed to the boat's compass resting in a binnacle that allowed the compass to remain level no matter what motion or angle the boat was sailing at. Don indicated a number on the compass and instructed me to keep the boat heading in that direction. Why? I thought, just before I looked up and saw the now very little boat was surrounded by a very big sea, the English Channel to be precise. Immediately images of Jaws, the Titanic and other assorted marine disasters invaded my panic stricken mind. We were at sea! Crap! Not sure if I was thrilled at the adventure or terrified as my knuckles turned white with the force of my grip on the tiller. Don was oblivious to my dilemma as he wandered about the boat pulling on this or adjusting that, all the while puffing happily on his pipe. I kept my eyes glued to the compass as I attempted to do two things at once, the first was stay on the course Don had indicated, the second was how long before I could visit the heads (*toilet*) without giving away the fact that I was about to crap myself.

After what seemed an age but was in fact just a few moments, my fear subsided and I began to delight in the scene about me and the new experience of being in control of a real boat on the real water, my yellow bath duck would be absolutely beside itself with jealousy. Soon I was standing in the cockpit with one hand nonchalantly on the tiller as my eyes took in the vast open space and the gently rolling swells of the sea. I even managed to steer safely away from a large cargo vessel that was heading into port, a mile long skyscraper on the water, least that is how it appeared to me on our now much smaller boat bobbing about on the water's surface. I knew that motor is supposed to give way to sail, however a humongous mass of steel weighing thousands of tons takes time to turn or shift its position on the water. When faced with a vessel that big, prudence demanded that I steer our miniscule craft quickly out of the way, that big damn ship was not going to stop for the likes of me, sail or no sail!

In truth we were not far from land and if I bothered to look behind me, I would have seen the shore, the cliffs and the hills and the small port from

43

which we had sailed. But I was having too much fun and looking back would only remind me that soon I would have to return home and leave this fascinating waterscape. Sadly and all too quickly the time passed and we headed back to the river and Don's mooring. I was thrilled with my first real trip on a magnificent yacht and vowed there and then to get my old bus out on the vast sea as soon as possible. Once back at the mooring, Don showed me how to catch the pick up line attached to his buoy with a boat hook. I am pleased to announce it was quite easy, Don manoeuvred his boat expertly and I barely had to reach more then a couple of feet to hook the line and tie it to the bow cleat. Then the routine tasks of securing the sails and tidying away all the paraphernalia that accompanied a sailing trip followed. In later years I would grow to dislike these chores immensely; however they were tasks that had to be done and after my first sailing trip I actually enjoyed them. When the responsibility fell upon me to organise the tidying and storing of my own boat before I could return to shore, the enjoyment of that first day quickly faded. I sailed with Don many times over the coming years, learning something new each time, but that was my first proper sail and I had loved it.

When I eventually arrived home, I was still buzzing with the thrill of the trip, so much so that my poor wife soon developed a headache and told me to shut up. I admit I went on a bit, and as I have already mentioned, my wife does not like boats. I suspected that while I raved about sailing, her secret wish was that I had fallen overboard.

Chapter Three: Bait box.

Work continued on the Lundy Mist though these were now only little jobs, much of the main tasks had been completed and my own little boat was soon declared sea worthy. However it appeared I personally needed a little more work. Mainly work on my common sense regarding a prospective life on the water, rather than under it. One morning as I was rowing my tiny tender across the river to the mooring of Lundy Mist, one of the local old boatmen thundered past in his huge boat he used to give river trips to holiday makers. I knew him very well as he was the person who laid my river moorings and tended them for me. He was not exactly the life and soul of the party but he was as honest and as forthright as humanly possible, a rare thing these days. Most of the people I knew on the river had at least one dubious streak in their personality. You know the type, retired bank robbers, tax avoiders, rich bankers retired at the grand old age of thirty five, ex-politicians and other assorted infamous celebrities. So finding a totally honest and trust worthy bloke was indeed strange. However, for as much as he was honest, so he was miserable and never held back when speaking his mind. As the tidal wave of his wake caused my boat to bob and roll, the old boatman peered down at me and offered what was for him, a pleasant greeting.

'Get that damn bait box off the water before you drown your bloody stupid self!'

These were his only words as he roared off in his boat, leaving me grasping tightly to the gunnels in an attempt to remain on board. Pondering his words and holding onto the contents of my stomach, I took my first sensible look at the boat in which I sat. In truth it could hardly be called a boat; in fact it was more suited to a small theme park lake, with kids splashing about happily in two feet of water. Only seven foot long with a blunt bow, not exactly an ocean liner and the way it bounced around on the river whenever another boat passed by, or even a duck for that matter, caused me to re-evaluate my passion for the *bait box*. If the old boat man considered my boat to be dangerous, who was I to argue and I decided to look for something more substantial when, and if I ever returned to shore alive.

Later that day I told my friend John what the old boat man had said, only to receive a mumbled reply, 'Why do you think I didn't like getting in the thing? I didn't say anything about it because I didn't want to hurt your feelings. You were so proud of that toy boat, but let's face it; it's not really suitable for a river which meets a tidal current. Time to look for something else I think. Actually I passed a boat on the way here that may do, let's go and take a peek.'

Huh! I thought, so not hurting my feelings over-rides my personal health or even my life? But John and the boatman were right, I needed a bigger boat. Now where had I heard that statement before? Oh that was it; those were the words spoken when the town sheriff first saw the shark called Jaws. Maybe I would get a bigger boat, and possibly a big gun, just in case.

Using my van, John and I set off in search of a more suitable vessel from which I could fall off. We found the boat about a mile from the river, sat amongst the weeds in the front garden of an elderly couple. Pinned to the bow was a sign that stated the boat was for sale and a price which I can no longer remember, but it could not have been expensive otherwise the wife would have drowned me herself. The boat in question was a good ten foot long with quite a wide beam, made of ply with a chine hull. All the wood appeared in good condition with no holes, which is always a bonus and it came complete with oars, rollicks and a few fenders. Quite a nice package in fact, I felt sure even the old boatman could not find fault with this craft, but you never know. Anyway I decided to take the risk and with the assurance that the boat was sound from John, I purchased it. How the heck I was going to transport it, I had no idea as it did not come with a road trailer and I did not own one myself. But I had a cunning plan . . .

As I mentioned at the start of these inane nautical ramblings, at the time I ran a landscape business and of course, I had an old van. So the next day I returned to the newly acquired boat and with the aid of some friends with plenty of muscle, we shoved the boat into the back of the van, well almost. We could not get the boat fully into the van, partially would perhaps be a better description, but with numerous ropes and string we managed to secure enough of the boat inside the van for transport. Least we hoped it was enough; I would have to avoid bumps, pot holes and policemen on the journey but hey ho and off we go. We travelled the huge distance of twenty feet before having to stop and retie the knots one of my friends had tied; it was obvious he was never a boy scout. In punishment we made the said offender travel squashed up in the back of the van holding onto the boat as an added precaution. It was not just his inability to tie a good knot that caused his expulsion alone; his more serious crime was because he had obviously indulged in several beers and a very hot curry the night before. The van smelt bad enough with petrol fumes mixed delightfully with the bouquet of rotting vegetation lingering from carrying garden waste. We did not need another fragrance percolating through the vehicle!

With only a few screams of agony from my friend in the back of the van, we reached our destination at the river. The drive had been very slow but the boat seemed fine. Manhandling it to my river side frappe, we exchanged boats and jammed the bait box in the back of my van, accompanied by a very disgruntled smelly friend. Off we set to my home where I would store the smaller boat in my front garden until I could find a mug . . victim . . sorry, a willing buyer. I knew I was taking a huge risk by dumping the boat in my garden, once the wife came home from work I was sure to be in trouble. But things worked out well and a chap turned up a couple of days later to purchase the tiny bait box as the boatman had called it.

The prospective buyer was a strange character who assured me it was just what he wanted. I will never forget his appearance, missing teeth, one wooden leg, an eye patch and a parrot on his shoulder, he was the local vicar. As it transpired the vicar was not going to use the boat for its intended purpose, the boat was destined to become a glorified flower tub on the grass verge outside his stately home, the vicarage. Our church was holding a village in bloom competition and he thought a flower filled boat would promote the competition nicely. I thought, *whatever*, and sold it to him. I left for work then, leaving him staring at his new acquisition and scratching his head. I had offered to transport the boat to its new residence in my van but he had declined my offer, thankfully. At the end of the day when I returned home, the boat had gone. It's a miracle I thought! As for my new tender, it proved to be a brilliant little boat, easily carrying three people and one small dog.

Work was now able to progress on the Lundy Mist and it was time to try it out, so life jackets on and Wills amended, off we set. John took charge as I was still learning and we stayed within the river for safety. The river was always quite busy so we concluded if we sank or got into any form of difficulties, someone would eventually come along and rescue us, we hoped. John began by showing me how to hoist the sails and lay out all the sheets so they would not tangle or trip us. Then the mooring line was released and off we slowly sailed, and I do mean slowly. It turned out neither of us had bothered to take notice of the weather. I had noted that no torrential rain or floods were expected that day but stupidly failed to noticed wind speed and direction indicated by the local weather forecast. As it turned out there was hardly any wind, so our first real test of the Lundy Mist was – becalmed!

We hardly moved, in fact if the tide was not flowing we would not have moved at all. John explained he was going to take down the jib and raise the genoa, a statement which absolutely dumbfounded me. Firstly I did not know I had such a thing, and secondly I had no idea what it was. As I watched from the safety of the tiller, John hauled down the jib and carefully laid it along the bow before dragging a grey and stained canvas bag out of the bow hatch. Obviously he had discovered it earlier and had the foresight to position it ready, clever guy old John. With experienced hands, John soon had this new sail attached to the fore stay and began pulling up the sail. Up went the genoa and almost immediate I could see it was larger than the jib. I was even more convinced when I saw the genoa reached a lot further back along the boat than the jib did, in fact it came back past the mast. How the heck was I supposed to steer the Lundy Mist when I could no longer see where I was going. Working his way back to the cockpit, John grasped the line (*still do not know what that was called*) and pulled the genoa tight. Almost at once we began to move faster, we could now even out pace a duck. But in truth the speed of the boat did increase and soon we were sailing, albeit somewhat sedately along the river.

Thankfully John took over the tiller and explained how one managed to sail when one's vision was blocked by a damn great white and green striped sheet. He instructed me in the use of a genoa or genny as it is often known and as soon as he considered me able, I eventually retook control of the tiller and we continued our maiden voyage on the Lundy Mist. As part of my lessons, John had me steer as near to either river bank as possible without causing a shipwreck. This he assured me was to make full use of the river's width and allow me to practice tacking and gibing, reefing and other such delightful activities with silly names that accompany sailing. There were many other boats moored or at anchor along the river so John had me manoeuvring around them as well as trying to get to grips with the sails. I swear he was having fun, watching my mad antics as I attempted to put into practice what little knowledge I had.

I tried to take it all in but sailing was so alien to me that I suffered several mishaps along the way. First I forgot to duck and received a nice lump on my head from the boom; I also did not see another small yacht heading straight for me and came close to a collision. I already knew that motor should give way to sail where appropriate but I was confused about sailing etiquette when faced with ramming another sailing boat. John explained it was all to do with the wind direction and launched into a lecture on the right of way in sailing. This was way too much for me, I was having enough trouble steering the thing to notice other boats on my blind side, I think even the QE2 could have come within striking distance without me seeing the damn great thing. I admit I still do not fully or even partially understand the rules of right of way in sailing; I tended to remain on my set course and hope to hell that the other sailor moved first.

I had quite a few near misses that day and to be honest, John expected this but his guidance kept us both safe, apart from one small mishap, that I almost feel ashamed to recall. The boat was sailing along nicely, the river was calm and the wind was slight. The birds were singing, the fish leaping and the sun was shining warmly. Everything was right with the world until a large boat decided to pass close to our port side a tad too fast. The couple on board waved cheerfully at us as they motored past and we waved back. Then their wake hit us! As I said, the other boat was going too fast for the six knot limit on the river so the wake was huge; it rushed against the Lundy Mist like a wall of water and sent it rocking furiously. This then was the reason behind my biggest accident on that day. I was holding a very hot cup of coffee at the time and the violent rocking caused the coffee to spill all over my lap. Mainly it spilled over my crotch and the effect was immediate. Up I sprang with a shout of pain and fury, my groin being boiled alive as I rushed to my feet and threw the now empty cup down, I sprang up so fast I forgot the low hanging boom and, crack! I hit my head again.

So now I had a sore aching head and boiled genitals. Shaking my fist at the now disappearing culprit and shouting some very choice words at their vanishing stern, I realised I had let go of the tiller. Quickly I reached down to grasp the wooden handle but alas too late. With a bump the Lundy Mist hit a large motor cruiser that was swinging lazily at anchor. No damage was done to either vessel but the sudden halt caused a bad tempered boat owner to fall flat on his backside in the cockpit. Who was the bad tempered boat owner? Me of course! My feet slipped on the damp cockpit floor and down I went, accompanied I might add by the peals of laughter issuing forth from my trusted old friend John. Luckily no one was aboard the motor cruiser and there were no other witnesses to my calamity other than a now helpless John. So that was the only painful mishap we encountered that day and with my privates rapidly cooling, we headed back to our moorings and home, mostly contented at the days practice.

Over what remained of that summer, I spent as much time as I could on the Lundy Mist, just trying to become more familiar with all the fixtures and fittings, what rope or sheet went where and did what, what cleat held what sheet and continued with the minor jobs that still required attention. I did not attempt to sail the boat, instead I would row the tender out across the river, climb aboard the Lundy Mist, and once the little jobs were done, mostly cleaning off seagull droppings, I would just sit gazing at the beautiful scenery about me. My eyes drank in the sight of the small hamlet that overlooked the tiny quay and slipway. The surrounding hills covered with fields and woods, the peacefulness of the lapping water against the hull and the variety of birds that called this stretch of water their home. I would spend hours just sitting on the Lundy Mist and watching the world around me, until a friend realised what I was doing. As a novice, I was unaware of a more dubious ritual practiced by many of the local boatmen and sailors. There I was, happily doing nothing with the sun on my face while the boat gently bobbed about on the water when a shout disturbed my peace.

'Hey, Lundy Mist. Can I come aboard?' called a voice I knew. Peering in the direction of the sound I saw Steve sat grinning up at me from his dingy. Steve was a keen boatman and lived very near me, so it had not taken long for us to become friends with a shared interest in marine activities.

'Hi Steve, yep of course you can. Do you need a hand?' I called back.

'Nah, tis fine. I'll just tie me tub onto one of yer stern cleats and I'll hop over. Here take this a minute will 'ee?'

Steve reached up and handed me a plastic shopping bag and from the feel of it, I knew what it held. In a moment Steve was on board the Lundy Mist and making himself comfortable on the cockpit seat opposite me.

'What cha doing mate?' he asked, 'Got problems?'

'No, just chilling and admiring the view. Tis lovely here.'

'Wife not with you then?' he asked while peering into the small cabin.

'No I'm on my tod.'

'Thought so. When a bloke takes it easy you can guarantee the missus ain't about anywhere,' chuckled Steve. 'ere, 'ave one of these.'

Still grinning, Steve handed me a can of cheap lager from the plastic bag before grabbing one for himself and lifting the pull ring to open it.

'What's this in aid of then?' I enquired.

'No reason really 'cept tis a bit of a thing we do 'ere. Probably a few more boys will be along soon, you'll see.'

Steve was tall and very thin; perhaps one could call him wiry but thin seemed a more apt description. Not much hair and what there was clung precariously to his head and severe greying was evident. A hand rolled cigarette hung from his lips and he some how managed to puff and drink at the same time. Almost before Steve had finished speaking there was a light bump as another small boat came alongside, followed by a voice calling, 'Hoy Lundy Mist. Can I join yer?'

In a moment another new acquaintance had appeared over the gunnels, again armed with alcoholic refreshment of the tinned variety. It was a chap named Wally, for reasons best known to him. Wally was a large red faced individual somewhere in his fifties.

Slightly long wavy white hair framed his round smiling face as he clambered into the boat and sat down beside Steve. Suddenly Wally stood up again and began pulling his own small tender closer to the Lundy Mist. 'Almost forgot.' He muttered as he reached down into his boat and came up with a small dog in his arms.

'Nearly forgot 'ee didn't I me old boy,' he said to the Jack Russell terrier in his grasp. So then there were three men and a dog in the boat, I am sure there is a story or rhyme about that somewhere. On my boat in the sun we all sat, well we men sat anyway, the little dog was happily sniffing around my boat. We rested and chatted for half an hour or so, talking about nothing in particular as we supped on the beverage thoughtfully supplied by Steve before starting on Wally's supplies. It turned out that this was rapidly becoming an ancient custom on this particular stretch of river. If one sat on one's boat while still moored, passing boatmen and sailors would drop by for a chat and frequently a drop or three of beer to pass the time. I will admit I enjoyed the experience greatly, feeling slightly sad when the time came for them and me to head back to the shore. Being a tidal river and on that day it was spring tides, we would soon be left high and dry upon the boat as the water disappeared beneath us. This would result in a long muddy walk back to shore and none of us wanted that. So by mutual agreement, it was decided we would continue our important discussion about nothing in particular in the pub on dry land.

There were many such gatherings on our local river and over the years I spent many a happy hour sipping beer with friends while sat in the sun shine on a boat in the middle of the river. Only once do I recall having a few too many sips and the rather eventful journey back to shore in my little rowing boat. Along with the river gathering regulars, the hamlet where I moored my boat was also a friendly place. I had quickly discovered while repairing and working on Lundy Mist, just how close and friendly the local boating community was. One only had to own a boat to join this faculty, the size, shape and cost of the boat held no value, several owned floating gin palaces while others risked the wrath of the river in boats that were no bigger than a bath tub, as indeed was my first dinghy I remember. Other boatmen had approached John and myself when we were spotted chucking nails, hammers and other assorted DIY implements around the Lundy Mist on the river bank, accompanied by a few choice words when a particular job was not going well, some even offered to lend a hand. In this world of personal space and unwillingness to get involved, it was a pleasant change to encounter friendly strangers who soon became friends. Sadly some visitors and part time sailors who appear for a fortnight once a year chose to remain aloft from such interaction and miss out on the camaraderie of the boating community. Within a month or two of working in the cold mud beside the river, we had gained many friends and even more advice on what we were doing right or wrong.

I soon realised that these boating people had a special way of remembering another. When a bunch of these boatmen gathered, describing a fellow or friend was always done via the name of their boat.

'Do you know that bloke who's got Seputus Sue . . . ?'

Or 'Him who owns that M. Celeste . . . . . ?'

Or 'You know 'im, he's got the Black P . . . . . '

It very quickly became apparent that in this community, people were known by the name of their boat and pity the poor fool who christened his boat, Little Dick! Both John and I picked up on this trend and began introducing ourselves as Lundy Mist before offering our actual names. Although somewhat a strange habit, it did help in reducing boat theft as each boat owner being known by the name of their boat made recognition easier when 'That bloke with Little Dick' was not the person attempting to sail off into the sunset in Little Dick. In other words the boatmen knew the name of each boat and the face of its owner, a stranger was spotted immediately.

There was one tale of attempted boat theft that caused much interest and merriment for some time, the tale being told and retold in pubs, harbours and small boats in the middle of the river. I actually met the chap involved so this story is true, honest. The chap was quite elderly, I am sorry but I cannot remember the name of his boat at this moment but that is not important. The story goes that the elderly chap who I shall call Jim, had decided on a days fishing. Going down to his dingy he found two men already making it ready to use. Hiding his surprise to find two men actually in the act of stealing his boat, he decided to play for time and have some fun. Being an elderly chap he could not physically take on the two younger and sturdy looking individuals, so standing on the river bank he smiled at the men.

'That's a good boat, is it yours?' he asked while still smiling and his hands stuffed deep into his pockets.

'Nah, tain't ours, it belongs to a mate and he said we could borrow it,' replied one of the thieves.

'Well tis a good boat, been looked after I see. Who's yer friend, never know, I may know 'im. I knows most folks who 'ave boats down 'ere.'

'Ah his name is . . . er, Dave, that's it, he's called Dave. He don't live round 'ere but he comes 'ere a lot. Do you know him? You must know Dave?' continued the same speaker while his accomplice continued storing their bags and making ready to move off.

Jim could hear footsteps coming up behind him along the narrow track that followed most of the river moorings along this section of the river, so he decided to up the stakes.

'Well I heard this was Jim's boat, who's this Dave then?' enquired Jim with a straight face.

'Actually mate, tis none of yer business who the hell owns this boat. We told you it was Dave's boat and we're borrowing it. Leave it at that will yer mate!'

It was clear the two men were growing concerned at this witness standing smiling down at them from the shore. Their actions became hasty and urgent, an obvious indication that they wished to be elsewhere.

'Well just to let ee know, my name is Jim and that's my bleddy boat!' exploded Jim as the footsteps grew very near.

'Yeah? Well what ee gonna do about it then? We're taking it so sod you!' growled the speaker with a snarl.

'Nope, `fraid it's Sod you!' Jim snapped back, 'think it's time you met me three boys!'

With that Jim stepped aside and the two thieves found themselves staring up at three of the biggest and meanest looking throwbacks of humanity that could still be classed as men.

I will not continue with the tale, suffice to add that those two gentlemen of dubious character did not make off with Jim's boat, in fact they did not make off anywhere other than hospital. I am led to believe their punishment dissuaded them from ever coming back to our small part of the country, when they had recovered of course, a recovery which took some time I was told.

Work on a boat never truly finishes, when one job is completed, another will rear its expensive head. So John and I were kept busy with small repairs, ongoing maintenance and of course, communal gatherings mid river. The old boatman passed me in my new tender on a number of occasions but failed to shout at me so I understood that the replacement boat was to his satisfaction. There were times when I wished I had an even bigger dingy, especially when attempting to ferry a friend and his wife from the quay over to their boat. Their own tender was in for repair and they desperately wanted to check over their yacht following yet another burst of torrential liquid sunshine well known during a British summer. As I was going out to the Lundy Mist anyway, I foolishly offered to give them a lift to their vessel which was moored not far from mine. It was a mistake that I would learn from. The couple were large, I mean very large and when they both climbed aboard, my poor little tender seemed to sigh as it sank deeper in the water under the weight, too deep for my liking. Then to my horror I realised the woman was actually wearing stiletto heels. On a boat? Good grief! My dinghy was only constructed of plywood, not reinforce steel, what the heck was she thinking? Dressed up in jewellery and high heels just to almost sink my small boat with her massive backside and cross a river to check over yet another boat. I still remember that trip, water lapping over the gunnels as I strained to row the extra weight over the water. Her husband was no different; his massive weight, perched alongside his ample wife caused the centre bench seat to bend in the middle. The weight one my boat was made even heavier by the collection of gold jewellery that adorned his vast body. Never was I so happy to see two people clambering off my boat, taking their tonnage and high spiked heels with them.

At last the time came for me to take Lundy Mist out to sea. The boat was ready and at that precise moment, so was I. It had been decided that John and I would take Lundy Mist out on the sea, just in the bay where we would be overlooked by a rescue service. Just in case you understand, I am not saying I expected a disaster but with my luck, one never knows. The chosen day arrived and I got down to my tender early, hoping to get as much done before John arrived, thus saving his old bones. I bundled all the sailing paraphernalia into my little boat and rowed across the river to the Lundy Mist. The morning was still and the water was calm, no sun shone on me that day but at least the British rain had paused for the moment. I looked forward to experiencing my first real adventure on my own boat rather than cadging trips out on friend's vessels. Once aboard I began the lengthy and often tedious chores of preparing the boat for sail. I stored all the important items such as tea, coffee, biscuits and cakes away safely and made sure the kettle was full and that I had gas for the Belling two ring cooker. When my priorities were satisfied, I proceeded to tackle the boat itself. I made ready the anchor in its position on the bow and even remembered to attach its rope to a suitable point. There is nothing more embarrassing than throwing your anchor overboard, only to watch the end of the anchor line disappearing into the water, and realising you had not secured it first. I did not always remember this minor but important fact.

Next I set up my antique depth sounder, there was no real reason as we were not challenging the ocean, but I had one so I was going to use it. The sails came next and I dragged them from the storage under the bunks and manhandled them towards the bow hatch. This was a delightful task, attempting to jostle three large sail bags in the very small and confined space of the cabin. Then it was up onto the deck where I struggled to pull the mainsail through the bow hatch and with fumbling hands, attached the huge great thing onto the main halyard. It is funny how a calm day will suddenly become breezy when one attempts such an operation as this. With much choice language, the mainsail was in place but left loose to flap in the breeze. I did not wish to begin spinning about on the mooring like an amateur while still within sight of shore. I admit I was indeed an amateur but I saw no reason to advertise the fact. Next came the jib, this at least was somewhat easier to manoeuvre through the bow hatch as it was smaller. The jib was also easier to attach to the jib halyard as it was attached via small simple clips. Again I left the jib loose as I trailed the jib sheets back towards the cockpit through the running cleats thoughtfully provided by the builder. The genoa I left just inside the bow hatch as I suspected I would not need it that day but chose to be prepared.

So now I was sat on the Lundy Mist under full sail but as yet I was going nowhere. I glanced at my watch wondering where John had got to, he was seldom late and I began to grow concerned. While I waited I turned my attention to my sleek, powerful and reliable outboard motor, my British Seagull. Who ever may have had the delight of having owned or still owns a Seagull will realise my description of the Seagull was not entirely accurate. The thing sat silently on the transom at the stern of my boat, innocently portraying a reliable source of propulsion that would safely power me out of any trouble with a simple pull of the starter cord. Yeah right! British Seagull outboard engines changed little in their design over the years they were manufactured and mine was no different. I think it was a Silver Century however it could well have been the forty plus model, they may have been the same for all I knew. Whatever the model, my Seagull looked like any other. A black fuel tank and silver flywheel atop a square motor and the long silver painted shaft reaching down to the propeller. The shaft had once been chromed or something similar but over the years paint had been used to cover the rust. A two foot piece of old cord served as the starter and a simple throttle lever situated on the steering arm controlled the speed. Unfortunately the infamous British Seagull halted production in the 1990's after losing the battle against more modern alternatives. However I believe the factory remains today, manufacturing spares and parts for the thousands of Seagull's still in use.

There was still no sign of John and I had to make use of the tide, so armed with no knowledge, a dubious Seagull and a very impatient personality, I decided I would attempt my very first solo sail. The day was overcast with a reasonable breeze blowing. I had no idea what the wind force was but as I was able to stand on deck without being blown off, it seemed fine to me. Checking the Seagull had enough fuel, I pulled the starter cord in order to motor off my moorings, I certainly did not have the courage to attempt using the sails to manoeuvre away from all the other craft moored around me. As usual the Seagull took a few pulls to start it, about five pulls on a good day, accompanied by sweat and swearing normally. Finally with a cough and a splutter it roared into life, and I do mean roar! The Seagull was never regarded as being a quiet engine. Swiftly untying the Lundy Mist from her mooring buoy, I slipped the motor into gear and set off towards the sea.

Chapter Four: Solo and scared.

At last I began my first solo trip. Admittedly I was not off around the world, but one's first solo sail is daunting and I was thankful I had chosen to wear brown trousers that day. The boat veered away from the safety of its moorings and the chugging Seagull pushed me through all the moored vessels with little mishap. Perhaps the day will turn out fine I hoped, there was only one way to find out.

With one hand on the tiller and the other on the Seagull, I steered the boat through the middle of the wide river. I needed to hold both the engine and the tiller because I could not set the Seagull to drive straight and nor could I do the same with the tiller, so I was stuck, resembling a contortionist with my hands going one way but my head and body attempting to go another. I did after all need to see where I was going, I find it always helps. No wonder I received some strange looks from other boat users. My heart was in my mouth because I really had no skills, knowledge or experience of sailing and there was a good chance I would make a stupid mistake and end up being nibbled on by fish. However I sailed on regardless, past other moored vessels, past boats coming in the other direction and past local landmarks that appeared strange when viewed from the water. Ahead of me and about half a mile away was a sharp left hand bend in the river, closely followed by a right turn. Of course I did not understand the significance of this and plodded on. On both sides of the river tree covered hills towered over me, yet another sign I was blissfully unaware of at that moment. Unaware of how the boat, tide and wind would react in a scenario such as this, I would find out.

Reaching a part of the river with no other craft about me, I decided it was time to raise the sails; the roar of the Seagull was getting on my nerves. Inexperience led me to believe I could sail on a bending and hill surrounded river and in truth, I was eager to try my hand at this sailing business. With the sails hoisted I tacked and jibed happily for a short while until I reached the first bend. Then all my grand hopes went swiftly to pot. The wind changed direction, the boat decided to head for the shoreline rocks and yes, you have guessed it, the damn Seagull would not start! I had not known that the wind would do strange things in certain landscapes and this bend was no exception. From a gentle breeze coming up river it suddenly seemed to swirl in all directions, I simply could not steer the boat, or rather I tried to steer but the damn boat ignored me and went off in the direction of its own choice.

Trying hard not to panic I rushed between the sails and the Seagull, righting my passage for a moment via the sails, then hurrying back to the engine, which did not start so back to the sails again. Everything was happening so fast and frantically that I really had no time to undertake lowering the sails or fiddle with the motor as the rocks grew nearer at each random puff of the wind. The sweat poured from me and a selection of swear words ripped constantly from my throat as I struggled to get the boat away from the rocks. I did not know if I was moving fast enough over the water to hit the rocks with enough force to cause damage, but I certainly did not want to find out. All too soon I was so close to the rocks that I was forced to grab one of the oars I had brought with me from my little tender and use it to push the boat away from those jagged black and very frightening rocks that loomed up far too close to my puny wooden boat. Each time I managed to sail the boat away from the rocks and out into clearer water, the wind began to blow me back. Every time I let go of the tiller to tackle the now much hated outboard motor, the wind pushed me towards the rocks at a speed that appeared alarming to me.

Finally I took a major decision and went for the Seagull, leaving the sails flap and take me where they would, ignoring the rocks and any stray mermaids in the vicinity, I grasped the pull cord, wrapped it around the flywheel and pulled. Nothing! Suddenly my mind cleared, and I reached down to turn the fuel tap on. I had turned the fuel off when I raised the sails and had forgotten the fact that a petrol engine will not work with no fuel. Another wrap and pull of the cord and the old Seagull roared back into life, unfortunately my bow was now pointing directly at the rocks. With a rumble of breaking wind emitting from my underpants and overpowering the roar from the engine, I yanked at the tiller and the motor handle, forcing the bow around and away from the dreaded rocks. At last I was free, for the moment. I steered the Lundy Mist back out in the centre of the river and gasped in great lung full's of air as I peered nervously at the right hand bend approaching fast ahead of me.

I let the sails go as loose as I could without actually untying them completely and continued on my unintentional suicide mission. In the swirling wind the boom slammed from port to starboard and back, forcing me to keep my head down or lose it. The sails themselves flapped noisily as I headed into the wind but I could not have cared less, at that moment I would have cheerfully ripped the things to shreds with my bare hands. But the motor was chugging along happily so I sank gratefully onto the stern seat and wiped my dripping brow. Although the weather was not overly warm, I was sweating profusely. I concluded that attempting to use the sails again while still on the river could be classed as foolhardy or at least damn stupid, so I allowed the old engine to push me towards the next bend. As it happened I navigated the second bend easily and the wide estuary of the port opened before me. I found myself now being rocked gently as I headed into the stronger tide of the harbour, I could see the open sea about half a mile or so beyond my bow.

Going through the huge port was another new experience. There appeared to be hundreds of other craft zooming to and fro about me, a huge cargo vessel creating a wake that hit my little boat like tidal waves.

Expensive yacht's, motor launch's, fishing vessels and ferries all scuttled about the river like huge Water Boatman insects fleeing hungry fish across the surface of a pond. Never before had I felt so small and as insignificant as I did while steering my tiny craft through the busy estuary and its harbour. It was a natural harbour formed by the water flowing through over millions of years. Coming down river the sides quickly opened up creating a wide almost oval space approximately a half a mile at its widest point, and roughly a mile from the initial widening of the estuary to the harbour mouth. On one side a small village nestled on the sloping hills that gently eased down to a short quay from which ferries scuttled to and fro. Opposite the village and across the wide harbour was situated a town, actually it was just a large village but the locals called it a town so who am I to argue. It was from this town and its slipways and quays that most mariners began and ended their trips, plus it was a main tourist attraction. The town stretched from the waters edge and on up a hill before disappearing into woods and farmland. An opening of perhaps two hundred yards in the circle of hills provided access to the ocean beyond, creating a natural harbour mouth, both points of the gap consisting of sharp black rocks, just to make things even more interesting for the hapless sailor, like me.

I had never sailed in such open water before, but let's be honest, I had never sailed anywhere and the space and activity of the harbour did little for my bowels. Desperately I tried to remember the rules of the road, or water if one wishes to be precise. Steering the Lundy Mist over to the right or starboard side of the river, I put on a brave face and waved back at the other sailors and boatmen that passed me from the other direction. None could see how terrified I was as my little craft made its way through the throng of assorted marine craft and the tall cargo ship that towered over me like a floating skyscraper. On the town quay and narrow roads I could see hordes of people enjoying their holiday by the water or locals simply going about their daily business. Seagulls, of the bird variety flew and swooped for each tasty morsel dropped or thrown by visitors who knew no better, occasionally diving down and tearing a chip or doughnut from unwary fingers while a solitary ice cream van played its tune to attract customers like the Pied Piper attracting children.

The harbour town appeared grey in the gloom of the overcast day, the small ancient buildings rippled up the hill away from the river, a church stood sentinel in the centre. Houses painted in all shades and colours of the rainbow while the uniform grey slate roofs gave the impression of a gigantic umbrella covering the busy coastal scene below. Narrow streets filled with people in all manner of dress, from shorts to jeans, mini skirts to frocks, all the normal attire favoured by the typical visitor. Locals could also be spied attempting to force their way through the ambling crowds as they made their way to and from their every day chores. Not able to take the time to browse each shop window or stare in fascination at a seagull that stared straight back at them, daring them to loosen their grasp on that pasty or pie wrapped in a white paper bag and held unsuspectingly in a hand. The harbour quay wall stood proud against the elements but faced constant erosion from the millions of sandaled feet that trod upon its surface each and every day of each and every summer. Small boats, dinghies and tenders lined the harbour wall, tied up and bobbing on the water as they patiently waited for their owners to take them out onto their intended environment.

While taking in all the sights of the port, I also kept a wary eye on the yachts and other sail boats entering the harbour, marking how they had their sails and how many sails they had hoisted. Again I did not realise that most sailors lowered their sails when entering a harbour, so I saw the reefed or lowered sails on the incoming vessels and took that as a sign of what I must do once I was free of the port and out on the sea. Onwards I drove through the busy port, avoiding all that deemed to come near my tiny vessel, and especially staying clear of those small boats flying about the harbour with way too many people on board. Pleasure boaters just like me or sailing crews most of them, though I did see many children piloting silly little dinghies with not a care for what other vessels loomed around them. I have always considered it strange how people who only visit the water for two weeks of the year consider themselves experienced mariners. But hell, let's be honest, who was I to talk; I had absolutely no idea what I was doing myself.

Suddenly the boat began to rock and pitch about alarmingly. I dragged myself from my contemplation of the boating community and took stock of my surroundings. I was out of the harbour and crossing through its mouth. At this point the water is always slightly rougher or so I had been told, and although I should have expected it, I had not. Grasping tiller, engine and buttocks tightly, I steered the boat straight out of the harbour and away from the land. Once away from the curved rocks that formed natural sea walls on either side of the harbour entrance, the sea began to calm and so did I. Slipping the motor into neutral gear, I had no intention of turning it off this time, not until I was successfully sailing anyway. I may be slow but I had learned that lesson. I reached out and pulled the mainsheet tight, nearly falling overboard in the process. One should never over reach on a boat as a soaking may result. With the sail tight it caught the wind and in a flash the Lundy Mist was heeling over so far that I panicked I was going to capsize. Remember I had never sailed the boat out on the sea before so I had not experienced how yachts keel over as they sail. Swiftly I loosened the mainsail and secured it loose enough to catch the wind without scaring the crap out of me. On the sea I had room to manoeuvre and make all my mistakes with no sharp rocks to cure any constipation. Next I pulled on the jib sheet and the boat launched itself forward with a totally unexpected turn of speed. Hell, I thought, I am really sailing.

Yes I was sailing but in truth I had little clue as to what I should do, so I peered about me and made sure there were no other craft or Chinese oil tankers in my vicinity and began to play. By play I mean I began experimenting with the tightness of the sails and the direction I steered the helm. I knew enough to know it was the wind that moved my craft over the water and not magic, so with no sorcery spells at hand I deduced some skill must be involved. Unfortunately they were skills I did not have but I concluded that I would either learn or drown. I was still wearing my life jacket and the bay around the port held a steady stream of traffic and I hoped I would be rescued swiftly and not end up as flotsam on the sea. However just in case a typhoon suddenly appeared or a Russian submarine chose to surface beneath me, I thoughtfully decided that sailing out to sea would not be such a wise idea. So instead I began to make my way across the mouth of the bay, thus remaining within sight of other vessels. Sailing to and fro across the bay near to the safety of the harbour and the rescue look post was one of my random intelligent decisions.

I turned the bow towards the starboard navigation light built high upon the cliff rock face and headed off towards it. The breeze that spun and confused me on the river was stronger out in the open bay and I found myself fighting the wind. If I loosened the sails any further I would most likely end up just floating aimlessly on the water with the sails flapping madly about me. I looked around and studied the sail set up of those boats accompanying me on my little excursion. Though none were near enough to worry me, I could at least see how they set their sails. It appeared that many had reefed their main sails but I also knew they were all much further out to sea than I was. I decided to lower the jib as it was too far away from my seat in the cockpit for me to scramble to quickly if I got myself into trouble. Letting the mainsail loose I dived into the cabin and poked my head up through the bow hatch to reach the jib. I certainly did not have the courage to attempt the walk over the deck to reach the jib, lowering it from the relative safety of the hatch made me feel slightly braver. I had remembered to untie the jib sheet before ducking through the cabin so all I now had to do was reach behind me and loosen the jib halyard on its cleat and allow the jib sheet to lower towards me. With one hand I lowered the halyard, with the other I pulled the jib sheet down into the hatch and bundled it in an untidy pile in the cabin bow. Already I could feel that the Lundy Mist had lost its forward momentum so closing the hatch once more, I hurried back to the cockpit to resume control of the vessel, a contradiction in terms but I still considered I had some control over the thing at that point.

Reaching the tiller I quickly glanced around to ascertain I was not about to be rammed and sunk by any stray aircraft carriers that I had not spotted before, or even a rabid dolphin out to get a name for itself. The sea about me was still clear however I realised I was now heading all too quickly for the rocks that formed the harbour wall. Pulling the mainsheet in to gain steerage, I pushed the tiller over and manoeuvred a gentle 360 degree turn towards the opposite side of the bay. The Lundy Mist behaved itself, amazingly, and I finally allowed myself to sit back and enjoy the ride. With the port on my left side and the open sea on my right, I moved serenely over the water at a pace that would not win any races but might avoid me doing anything rash in panic. For the next couple of hours I sailed to and fro across the bay, adjusting the mainsail occasionally if more speed was required to avoid another vessel entering or exiting the harbour, or a loosening of the sail to bring me to a halt if I could not get out of the way in time. If I am totally honest, I must admit that day has to go down in my memories as one of the best. Never had I felt so at one with the elements and the earth, yes I know sailing across a bay is hardly a seagoing adventure, but it was my first and I loved it.

Chapter Five: Suicidal Seagull.

At last the time came for me to head back into the harbour and attempt to reach my moorings before I lost the tide. That is the one drawn back of having a tidal mooring; one can get stranded very easily if one is not careful and constantly aware of the tide times. With some regret I pointed the bow at the harbour entrance and began the journey home. While I slowly sailed towards the harbour I took the time to refuel and start the Seagull engine, I was going to be prepared this time. Thirty minutes later I was inside the harbour and once again surround by craft going in all directions. I released the mainsheet and began turning the handle that turned the boom and rolled down the mainsail, a task made easier in the space of the wide harbour. The Seagull was put into gear and I chugged upriver towards safety, and a much needed drink in the small hostelry that stood proudly overlooking the river adjacent to my mooring buoy. As I motored through the harbour I was constantly hailed or waved at by friends and fellow sailors but dared not risk attempting to either stop my craft, or try and manoeuvre close to their vessels for a chat and a can of beer. All too soon I passed through the harbour and found myself once more heading for those two troublesome bends in the river.

The first bend was negotiated with relative ease. I only had to avoid the cross river ferry which plied its trade from one side of the river to the other without a care about any passing traffic. Unless the passing traffic happened to be a huge cargo ship, then the ferry wisely allowed it to pass by before continuing on its endless journeys across the river. Of course the ferry would not stop for a lonely sailor aboard a small yacht and I was forced to slip the engine into neutral and drift on the water while the ferry smugly made its way across. Round the first bend which was still quite wide with no mishap, I began to feel confident that I would navigate the second bend with the same level of ease, and lo and behold I did. Yep it surprised the heck out of me as well. Without the hindrance of the sails and with the Seagull pushing me along at a steady pace, I rounded the bend and continued up river towards the mooring. I could not believe my luck or perhaps it was simply an occasional spark of intelligence, I could not say but that day I learned not to attempt sailing round those bends ever again.

Once that horrible bend in the river that had tried its damnedest to sink my boat on my outward trip was behind me, the water stretched straight and clear ahead of me. Surely nothing could go wrong now I thought as I settled more comfortably on the stern seat and watched the river banks and wooded hills pass me by on either side. I positioned the boat over on the starboard side of the river, close but not too close to the bank. I saw several other craft making their way up or down river and I noticed most kept their craft either in the middle of the river or further over to the bank now on my port side. I had no idea why they should do this, as far as I knew, I was following the rules of the water correctly and by staying over to my right or starboard, I was keeping out of everyone's way. I continued in blissful ignorance, watching the cormorants dive for fish, kingfishers glowing blue and orange while perched on overhanging branches and herons wading in the shallows. My attention drifted, lulled by the dull mutter from the Seagull and the sound of my wake flushing out behind me as I sat in peace upon my boat, the Lundy Mist. But peace is a fickle visitor and seldom lasts.

Suddenly and for no apparent reason, the Seagull engine decided it had behaved long enough and leaped from the transom. One moment it was chugging along happily with its two clamps gripping the transom tightly, the next it was heading for the water! It was an obvious attempt by a tired old engine to change its career and become the first ever British Seagull scuba diver as it headed, still roaring with life, towards the water. Luckily I still held onto its throttle handle and despite the fact that the damn thing caught me by surprise and nearly dragged me overboard with it; I managed to maintain my grip on it. Holding onto a throbbing engine while leaning overboard in a state of shock is no easy feat and I very nearly let go. I knew if I did, I would never be able to retrieve it from the river bottom and I was determined to retain my grasp. Early that day I may have happily thrown the damn thing overboard, but now I strove to save it, not because it was a reliable and trustworthy outboard motor, no it was because if the thing drowned I would be out of pocket. I had bought the motor and I could still sell the motor if it annoyed me further, but being fifteen to twenty feet under water would make a sale somewhat difficult.

With an aching arm I managed to manhandle the vibrating machine up from the water's surface, high enough to prop it on top of the transom and reach the throttle to turn it off. I was extremely surprised that the engine had continued to run, anyone who has owned a Seagull will know that it does not take much for them to stop running, but this stupid thing kept going! At last with the engine now turned off I loosened the clamps and once more set it in place on the transom before tightening the clamps once more, with an extra twist this time, I did not want the thing attempting to swim again. The ambitious Seagull firmly attached to the boat once more, I grasped the pull cord and wrapped it around the flywheel with the obvious intention of restarted it and continuing my journey home. Yeah right, I should have known better. Of course the damn thing would not restart, that would be too much to hope for. I had just saved it from a watery scrap yard and how did it repay me? By refusing to start of course!

After many rewinds and pulls on the flywheel I gave up, I was shattered after a morning of avoiding rocks, a day's sailing and now a kamikaze outboard engine. With a curse and a slap which hurt me much more than the engine, I sat down and contemplated my future. I was still floating nicely on the river a safe distance from the shoreline and there were no moored vessels within my immediate vicinity that I could collide with. Any passing craft could damn well steer around me, I was not moving and I did not care. A few moments of self pity followed before normal service resumed and I decided upon a course of action. Standing up in the cockpit of Lundy Mist, I raised my arms up into a 'Y' shape, the international marine signal of distress and hoped that one of the passing craft would see me. Some did see and waved at me, obviously morons who had no knowledge of nautical signals who decided I was simply waving at them for fun. But then a small open boat approached and a young boy aged under ten years of age I think, saw me and made whom I assumed was his father aware of me. At first I thought the father was going to follow the other sheep and wave at me, however I could see his son was persistent and the boat turned towards me.

'What's up mate?' called the man.

'My engine won't start and I can't get back to my mooring,' I replied through cupped hands as their little craft was still some distance away. I was grateful he did not suggest I put my sails up, as many wannabe sailors would have.

With a slight nod of understanding, the man brought his craft over and alongside mine, with some skill I might add. I quickly flung out some fenders and made ready a long rope. I knew if I used his rope then he would be entitled to claim salvage rights over my vessel, or so I had been informed by those in the know. Not that he would I thought, most boating people are only too happy to help a fellow in distress without calculating percentage figures of salvage, though I admit, I did know one infamous boatman that would have. Drawing alongside I explained what had happened and the man nodded again.

'Seagull?' he enquired.

'Yep!' was all I needed to say.

Together we tied the Lundy Mist alongside his boat at the stern and bow. We chatted politely as we worked and he did admit that he was about to just wave back at me. It was his son who recognised my signal and insisted his father check me out. A clever boy that, I concluded, much more clued up and intelligent than the armada of fair weather sailors who had passed me by with a wave and carried on their way, oblivious to my plight. My thoughts were not entirely generous or forgiving towards them at that moment.

It turned out that the father and son rescue team were actually heading down river to the harbour. By stopping to rescue me, they were forced to double back on themselves, a fact that made me feel all the more grateful and humble for their assistance. Once securely tied together, the father started his little four horse power Yamaha outboard and off we set up river towards my mooring. We continued to chat over the sound of his engine and while I worked furiously on my embarrassingly old British Seagull.

'I wouldn't bother with that,' stated the father, 'we'll be back at your mooring soon and you can hit it with a hammer then.'

'It's OK, I'm just trying to figure out what made the thing try to jump overboard. I couldn't see anything on the water but there must be a reason,' I explained.

We chugged on together and I learned the father's name was Phillip and his son was named Kyle, he was only nine years old but saw more with his young eyes than most adults do in their entire life time.

The pair had been heading down to the harbour just as a trip out; they were not in a hurry and were happy to help out. I continually thanked them until Phillip told me firmly to shut up. I was still fiddling with the Seagull when Phillip appeared to have an epiphany.

'Where were you on the river when it happened?' he suddenly enquired.

'Roughly where you found me, why?'

Phillip thought for a moment before explaining further. 'Well I believe there are nets under water in that spot. Local fishermen bring their catch in live and store them in net enclosures until they are ready to harvest them. I wonder if you caught the engine on one of the nets. Most other sailors avoid that side of the river because of the nets there.'

'I suppose it's possible, but I found no trace of netting on the prop when I fished it back on deck. Actually now I think on it, I didn't really examine the propeller; I was too busy trying to remain on board myself. I'll have a look when we get to my mooring. That's a good suggestion though. I've given it some thought but in my present state of mind, all I could think of were a randy Neptune or nomadic Great White shark playing tricks on me by nibbling at my propeller.

I suspect your suggestion is closer to the mark. Thanks.'

During the joining of the two boats and the initial part of our journey, I had explained to Phillip that this was my maiden sailing trip and described my frantic battle to get round the two river bends without becoming a submariner myself. Phillip it turned out; was an experienced sailor and owned a sloop himself. He recognised my inexperience and offered me advice on what to do if I ever found myself in that situation again. I was grateful but I had no intention of going through that again, not without a crew and a lifeboat standing near by.

I was still trying to start my engine in the hope that I could continue to my mooring under my own power and allow Phillip and his son to get on with their own planned trip. Phillip frowned and suggested I did not need to bother as we were almost there. Suddenly within a few feet of my buoy the obnoxious machine spluttered into life once more. I did not know whether to cheer at my success or swear at the thing for taking so long to start. But then we arrived and I left the engine running in neutral while I used the boat hook to grasp the lift strop from the buoy and slip the loop over my bow cleat. I was safely moored up once again and I will admit, I was relived to be there, back in the river and tied up next to my small tender.

We untied both vessels and Phillip and his intelligent son Kyle set off down river to continue their own excursion towards the harbour. I knew it would take them a good hour to reach the harbour and I was concerned that they would run out of daylight on their return trip. However Phillip stated he held no such concerns for night time boating, in fact he had decided both of them would stop off by the harbour quay and go ashore for a meal before returning, a statement which obviously pleased his son. I offered my thanks for the thousandth time and waved them off on their way. I was alone again and found myself staring in confusion at an outboard engine that was still chugging away as if nothing untoward had happened. Damn thing!

For the next hour or so I undertook all the normal routine jobs required when settling down a vessel on its moorings. Chores such as securing the sails in sail bags and stowing them in the cabin or tying down the mainsail on the boom to ensure it did not come unravelled and flap away happily by itself. I tied all the sheets tightly to the mast and also ran a short line between the shrouds so they would not rattle in the wind. As well as the shrouds, I also tied short lengths of cord around the mast in two places, thus stopping the main and jib halyards from slapping against the mast and annoying the local residents throughout the night. I unhitched the anchor from its bondage on the bow and stowed it below before pulling a net over the cabin and deck in a vain attempt to stop the flying variety of Seagull using my boat as a bedroom and toilet. The net was a simple garden type, used for growing peas and beans or for covering those precious strawberries from ravenous birds. I only needed to protect my boat from the bowel end of the birds.

Finally I turned my attention to the still running outboard motor sitting smugly on the transom. I closed off the fuel and stopped the engine before tipping it up by pulling the flywheel towards me so the propeller was up out of the water. There it was, a tight knot of fish netting wrapped around the blades of the propeller. I was not sure if I had caught the motor on one of those nets Phillip spoke about, or if I had picked up a free floating section of net during my travels that day. But either way; the netting would have to come off and better to do it now rather than tackle it on my next visit to the boat. Without a thought I reached down and grasped the main shaft of the outboard and swiftly recoiled back, whipping my hand off the still very hot shaft. I had stupidly forgotten that the exhaust travels down through the shaft on a Seagull and I had only just turned the engine off. Of course it was going to be hot! How I hated that engine at that point, even though it was me at fault. Stupidity being my most prolific genetic trait it seems. Leaning over the stern I drove my sore hand into the cool water of the river and prayed there were no vicious Piranha swimming below in search of a toasted morsel.

Once cooled to a suitable degree of pain, I pulled my hand from the water and reached further down the engine, grasping one of the propeller blades this time. I held tight but then realised I was at full stretch so although I could get a firm hold of the offending netting; I had no leverage with which to pull the netting off. I admit my intelligence, what little of it I possessed, was rapidly running out, I had used up my total allotted number of brain cells that day and now I could not think properly. Nothing unusual there so I carried on regardless. I stood up and scratched my head in confusion, how was I going to reach the netting with enough dexterity to remove it I wondered. I continued to stare at the water and my little tender bobbing along behind the Lundy Mist for some moments while I contemplated this dilemma. At last someone turned the light bulb on in my head and I realised I could use the tender to float around the stern of the Lundy Mist and thus remove the tangle of netting in relative comfort. Blimey, a good idea at last, I even surprised myself.

So pulling the tender alongside, I clambered into it and by walking my hands along the sides of the Lundy Mist; I made my way to the stern and the entrapped Seagull. Of course once in position, I remembered my knife which sat in readiness – on Lundy Mist. Once more I traversed the freeboard, climbed back up on board, retrieved the knife and reversed the whole journey back to the stern via the tender. Tying the tender front and back to the port and starboard cleats on Lundy Mist, I was finally able to attain free access to the propeller and its coat of netting. Quickly I sawed through the plastic or nylon or what ever the heck it was made of and threw the resulting mess onto the deck of Lundy Mist. I was not going to put it back in the water for some other poor schmuck to become entangled in; I knew for sure that schmuck would be me anyway.

Once the Seagull was completely free of netting I returned to the Lundy Mist and continued the assortment of chores required to make safe a boat for mooring. Leaving the Seagull propped out of the water, I used a plastic bucket to cover the engine and flywheel, no expense spared here. I ensured the fuel tap was in the off position, a task I always remember, it is the opposite task I forget, turning the damn fuel on again! Finally all the tidying up, storing, stowing, attaching, removing and securing chores were completed and my last action was to slide the 'wash board' doors into place over the cabin entrance and I was done. Wearily I climbed down in the tender, untied from the Lundy Mist and began the short row back to shore. I had enjoyed my very first solo sail but more importantly, I had learned many lessons. I hoped I would remember them, but some how I doubted it.

Chapter Six: Lessons.

I may be what is termed a slow learner in regard to the sport of sailing but one lesson I did learn was not to attempt any more solo sea trips anytime soon. From that day on I only ventured out to sea when accompanied by an experienced sailor. Sometimes I enjoyed the excursions out on the open water, other times I was extremely glad the Lundy Mist had a small toilet on board and numerous buckets.

On one particular trip with an acquaintance of a friend, I learned that not all sailors seek the gentle breeze and the relaxing swell of the sea; some sailors think they are racing drivers. The acquaintance called Johnny offered to accompany me out sailing one day. I eagerly agreed as I still wished to sail as much as possible and learn what little my brain could handle. Off we set down river towards the harbour and the sea. We used a newly acquired second hand and rather old Mercury four horse power engine this time. I had now given up on the Seagull. Johnny suggested we attempt to use the sails on the river journey but I declined, I was not going through that again, so we motored. Once in the vast space of the harbour, Johnny raised the sails while I controlled the outboard and kept us free of collisions and threaded my way through all the other craft dashing about the harbour. Out onto the sea and the motor switched off, Johnny took charge of the helm while I acted as cabin boy and made us each a mug of tea. I was looking forward to sailing Lundy Mist with someone who actually knew what they were doing.

I was mistaken. Suddenly the boat leaned over alarmingly, or at least it alarmed me. Rushing back onto deck with tea slopping everywhere, I peered about me convinced we had encountered a tidal wave or were being attacked by a Kraken or had hit some other sea going vessel. However the sea was empty, in fact it was empty for at least a half mile around the Lundy Mist, so what had caused the violent lurch over to one side? I turned my attention to Johnny who was grinning like a manic as he stood holding the tiller and mainsheet, a maniacal image heighted by his shoulder length dark hair streaming out behind him in the wind and the wild gleam in his eyes. It was quickly apparent he was responsible for Lundy Mist attempting suicide by capsizing.

Johnny was a tall dark and handsome guy, the type all we other ordinary blokes hate on sight. Wide shoulders, narrow waist, brown eyes and always a sure hit with the ladies. Johnny was dressed in a canvas smock favoured by many sailing types, worn blue jeans and a small woollen hat perched upon a thick head of hair. Why the heck had I accepted his offer I did not know.

'What's happened?' I screamed above the rush of the wind.

'Nothing, this is how you should sail, fast!' was his unsatisfactory reply.

'But we're going to tip right over! Look how far the boat is leaning, the water is almost over the gunnels!'

'Nah, this is nothing. The keel will keep us from tipping over and we need as much wind in the sails as possible. No good hanging around, we need more speed,' declared Johnny as his grin opened to revel perfectly even white teeth. I decided I hated him even more at that moment.

To say I was unconvinced by his boatmanship skills would be an understatement. I feared for my old wooden boat in the hands of this would be pirate. What the heck had I let myself in for? I pondered as I reached for my life jacket and hurriedly tied it around me. For the next hour or so, Johnny threw my old sloop about the water like Ben Ainslie sailing to escape the clutches of a shoal of frustrated mermaids. Unfortunately the craft Ben Ainslie used were far more suitable to sharp manhandling and thrashing speed than my plywood Caprice that had seen better days. My old boat was almost standing in its beam ends while the green sea rushed past less than an inch from where my fingers tightly grasped the gunnels. My lovely shiny varnished seats quickly became a health hazard as with every lurch of the boat, I slid off into the gangway. The mugs of tea were forgotten but they were empty now anyway. The tea itself was swilling to and fro in the gangway as Johnny tacked and beat this way and that, seemingly in an attempt to break the sailing speed record with a plywood boat and a terrified crew member. With shouts of *'lee ho'* or *'hard-a-lee'* each time I was sent flying across from one side to the other as the nutter at the helm changed direction, often nearly taking my head off as the boom swung like a pendulum with each manoeuvre. Everything I had caringly stowed in the cabin now flew about as if thrown by an angry poltergeist, shelves emptied and the cabin floor resembled a landfill site. I was certainly not enjoying the experience, thrilling though it may have been. I was simply too scared of what the lunatic would do next to enjoy the raw challenge of man against the ocean. I prayed for the trip to end and after a torturous period during which I fully expected Johnny to morph into a scaly demon with fins and an evil laugh, the tide turned and the time for us to return Lundy Mist to her berth arrived. One last frantic surge towards the harbour mouth preceded the command to loosen sails. In all truth, I have never before or since, untied sheets and halyards as fast as I did that day. The comforting mutter from the Mercury was a sound from heaven, I had returned to a safe place, motoring along sedately back to the river. I was so relieved when we finally returned to shore, so relieved I almost, I repeat, almost got down on my knees and kissed the ground. I never again asked Johnny to accompany me; I was in no hurry to meet Neptune face to face.

My old friend John still tried to teach me the finer points of sailing on a regular basis, but he refused to take an idiot like me and an old boat like the Lundy

Mist out to sea. He firmly stated that although he had sailed much of his life and felt confident in his abilities, with his advanced years he did not feel the same way about being responsible for me or my boat. I did not argue for I had grown to understand that John had a very wise head on his old shoulders and if he considered the open ocean too much of a challenge, I was happy to believe him. A belief strengthened following my experience with Johnny. So we did all our sailing on the river itself, which was actually quite difficult and therefore a much better learning venue than sat at the tiller at sea. Once the sails are up and the course direction decided, sailing can be quite boring, unless one is in a race or has Johnny at the helm that is. Sailing on the river required constant manoeuvring, tacking, jibing, and pushing off rocks with the boat hook and the occasional can of beer with passing boatmen. These lessons were strenuous but worthwhile and eventually I could steer the boat confidently and even set and trim the sails without any overriding stupidity. Even my young son James began to accompany us as we sailed up and down, and back and forth across the river, avoiding other craft, mooring buoys and rampant sea birds. I finally began to learn how to sail, my son learned faster.

I did go out to sea on Lundy Mist not long after my horrendous trip with Johnny, however this time is was with my old friend Don, a more laid back person, in no hurry to get there, where ever *there* was. Don had sailed around many coastlines in his time and he had wisdom about him that I found reassuring. The usual routine of preparing a vessel for sail ensued one bright morning. Sails up but loose, anchor mounted in readiness on the bow, Mercury purring away to itself and not a typhoon or Belfort Scale in sight. Sailing with Don could not be more opposite to the fear and panic that resulted from a trip with Johnny. Don certainly knew his stuff and instructed me calmly as we ventured down river to the sea. There is nothing much that can be said about my day's sailing, all went as expected, the Lundy Mist behaved herself, no water came over the gunnels and only I sat on my backside when I intended to sit on my backside. I did learn a lot from Don, but I knew that he knew that I knew that he knew I still had much to learn. If you understand me that is!

Several hours later with the Lundy Mist back at her berth, Don invited me to spend a day sailing on his own vessel. Of course I jumped at the chance; Don had a Contessa 26, a lovely sleek and fast sloop with a red hull which suggested it would fairly glide through the water. The following weekend I set off to meet Don on the quay where we boarded his small inflatable dinghy and headed off to where his boat was moored. Don kept his boat in a deep water mooring, which is a mooring that does not dry out at low tide like mine did; hence we used the inflatable to reach it. Climbing aboard his craft was like entering a Rolls Royce after exiting a Ford Escort, the difference was amazing. Gleaming superstructure with not one dollop of seagull mess anywhere, a warm wood varnished cabin complete with bunks, galley, heads, sink and all the comforts of home it seemed. Although not a large boat, its shape gave it the appearance of being long and fast, a sports car in opposition to my old bus.

We sailed all day with not one single mishap, a fact unheard of in my short experience. I even had time to trail a mackerel line over the stern and land a bucket full of the fish for us to share. I think Don took pity on me as he watched my childish enthralment as the yacht slid through the water like a knife, so much so that he asked if I would like to join his racing crew. So Don could sail fast if the situation demanded I discovered. He went on to explain that most weekends during the summer months the harbour authorities organised yacht racing in the bay and he regularly took part. He had two other crew members but due to work commitments, often only one would be available, so having a third, even if somewhat useless crew member would be a great help. Previously I had only witnessed sail racing on telly from the comfort of an arm chair so the idea of rushing around the deck, leaning dangerously overboard to counterbalance the force of the wind in the sails, dragging on ropes and swinging from the rigging gave me pause for thought, After a second or two of contemplation at least, I readily accepted his invitation with a reminder that what I knew about sailing held less content than a politicians speech. Don suggested I crew at the very next race, to which I agreed. He immediately stepped up the tempo of the vessel and began showing me some of what I would be expected to do.

Race day dawned clear and blue, but true to the British climate, by the time Don, myself and Ted his other crewman, reached the starting point, the weather had most certainly taken a turn for the worst. I keep waiting for the race to be called off, me being a fair weather sailor; I was not keen on the height of the waves or the low dark sky above me. However Don and his fellow competitors were made of sterner stuff and no one even considered delaying the contest, so the race was on as they say. My job was basically mobile ballast, I had to dive across the boat and hang onto the side of the boat that was uppermost, acting as a counter weight. Strangely enough, although I found myself staring at the water as it washed past and occasionally licked over the gunnels, I did not experience the same level of fear that I had suffered under Johnny's helm. Don and his mate Ted went about each tack, each turn and each manoeuvre with such calm and skill that I no longer felt at risk of drowning, not too much risk of drowning that is.

The starting gun fired and off we shot, in a totally different direction to all the other similar classed boats in our race. I looked over in question at Don as he sat with one hand grasping both tiller and mainsheet, the other holding a smoking pipe to his lips. He understood my confusion and explained that in a sea race, each vessel has to pass around strategically placed marker buoys along the route, however each boat was allowed to plot its own course, making best use of wind and conditions for his or her vessel. Don was heading out to sea so he could turn and run at the first buoy, hoping the speed gained on a dead run would push him into the lead. A dead run is when the boat is sailing directly away from the wind, or in other words with the wind blowing from behind the boat. His tactics worked and we gained a small lead on the first leg, only to lose it again on the second leg. For much of the time I was sat on the free board with my legs dangling into space over the side, only moving, and rapidly at that, whenever Don changed direction because if I stayed where I was, I would be under water. Not something I fancied as a pastime, so when Don heeled the boat over I rushed to the opposite side, or should I say I clambered carefully but with all due haste to the opposite deck and took up my perch over the side. The race was exhilarating and I watched both Don and Ted as they constantly tightened or let loose the sails, hoisted the genoa when the situation called for extra speed and literally flew around each marker buoy with barely inches to spare. At one stage Don let me take the tiller but my apprehension at doing something wrong and my lack of faith in my abilities soon lost us ground and Don had to take over once more. Ted also took a turn at the helm but he knew far more than I so no time or position was lost. I admit that while I had the tiller and when Don instructed me to keep the mainsail as tight as I could, with each lurch or further heel over, I unwittingly slacked my grip, causing the wind to billow out of the sails and resulting in a speed reduction. Subconsciously I desperately wanted to get the vessel upright again, which of course was not the way to win a race.

Finally we rounded the last buoy for the last time and the gun sounded again as we crossed the finish line. We came second in our class but I am sure if Don had not allowed me to man the tiller, we would have come first. However Don was gracious and did not mention the fact. In truth I think he simply enjoyed the race, winning or losing was not his major goal. Passing through the harbour Don waved up at the Yacht club and received a wave in return. Good practice and good manners Don informed me when I questioned his action, let's them know we are happy with the race and that we are okay. I considered this and concluded that if we were not okay, a distress flare or Mayday would be more appropriate than a hand wave, but I said nothing.

I crewed for Don many more times after that and we even won the odd race I am pleased to say. Not too shabby for a nautical novice I felt.

Don was a keen sailor and was always on the look out for a bigger and better boat. One day he called me and asked if I would like to go out on his new boat. I agreed and met him at the quayside with anticipation. Climbing into his inflatable dinghy, we set off to his deep water berth down river. The day was overcast and the wind stirred the water, making the surface choppy and restless, it was an uncomfortable ride in an inflatable. I mentioned my concerns to Don but he expressed little worry and tried to reassure my little troubled mind. Don informed me he had listened to the radio before coming out and the Shipping forecast had stated that there would be a six foot swell and a force six wind, nothing to worry his Contessa. Maybe not the Contessa but it sure worried the heck out of me. Changing the subject, Don explained on route that he had bought a Contessa 32 from a friend who had been desperate to sell for personal reasons which he did not expand on. His description of the new vessel meant nothing to me of course, being ignorant of the makes and styles of boat. I understood it would have sails, be larger than Lundy Mist and would float - hopefully. So I played along with his enthusiasm and waited to see the thing for myself. After a bumpy ride over the half mile or so it took to reach Don's new pride and joy, I got my first look at the vessel. It was as the name suggests, thirty two foot long with a wide beam of about nine and a half foot. It was a monohull design and the normal Bermuda sloop rigging littered the skyline above it. Don informed me that the Contessa 32 had been designed in the 1970's and had a fin and skeg keel, whatever that meant, I certainly had no clue.

The hull was coloured white which matched the white superstructure and had pale blue anti-slip sections. The mast appeared massive to me, not being experienced in such matters, and I prayed I would not have to scale the thing to fix any rigging or remove any low flying aircraft. Once aboard, Don gave me the delighted owner tour and I must admit, I was impressed, I had seen smaller and less luxurious caravans, and a few residential homes as well. The cabin was all clad in a rich varnished wood with space to spare. Beside the two sofas' that doubled as bunks, there was a small head or toilet in landlubber language, a shower, cooker, sink and a folding galley table, which also folded down to make bunks. A chart table and one small quarter berth completed the interior. Over all it was a beautiful craft and I could acknowledge Don's pleasure.

On deck the Contessa appeared much like any other sailing vessel, sheets and halyards lay along the cabin roof and the deck sides, small cleats and other assorted catches and blocks lay in wait to trip the unwary passenger while awaiting use in securing the appropriate rigging. I apologise for not naming these cleats and blocks correctly, but in truth I was still learning what they were all called. Finally a small fifteen horsepower engine hid from view beneath the cockpit with the starter and relevant controls under the port side cockpit bench. I know this because Don told me, however I never did see these controls which would cause some concern and will be explained further on in the tale. Don pointed out where the controls were but turned away to describe something else before I could shift my position to see what he was talking about. I decided it would be unlikely that I would need to start and use the engine, like I have mentioned several times, I was an inexperienced sailor.

Chapter Seven: Rough Weather

The first job I had to undertake when safely aboard the new Contessa was to clear the plentiful helpings of seagull droppings that splattered the decks and cockpit area. Don always insisted on a clean vessel before setting off anywhere. Although it was a loathsome task, I both understood and agreed with this practice, there is nothing worse than manoeuvring about a craft and placing one's hand or butt in a pile of bird poo. It does spoil the day somewhat and can lead to a larger than usual quota of rum, for medicinal and antiseptic purposes you understand.

While I worked as chief sanitation officer, Don set about readying the vessel for sea, calmly moving about setting the rigging, lifting fenders and mounting all the electrical paraphernalia that assists the modern sailor. Finally we were ready and the Contessa glided away from its berth, pushed along by the healthy sounding engine. Even with all his sailing experience, Don had no intention of attempting to sail around those two notorious bends in the river. It was a great pity I had not thought to speak to him before my eventful first solo trip. With smooth ease he steered the vessel through the other moored craft along our route, round the left and then the right hand bends and into the harbour. There was no fear or concern on his face as he chatted happily between waving at those sailors and boatmen he knew. Clouds of grey smoke issued forth from his old pipe like a factory smoke stack and matched the grey skies. The only time the pipe was removed from his lips was when an amateur sailor, Cornish smuggler or nautical idiot strayed too close on the wrong heading. Marine craft pass on the water port side to port side. Unfortunately the inexperienced or completely ignorant boater wrongly assumes that the rules of the water are the same as the rules of the road. In Britain I mean of course, some other countries drive on the weird side and some simply follow their noses. Although we remained to the right or starboard side of the river, numerous small craft piloted by biped lobsters tried to force their craft through the space between the Contessa and the river bank. This action guaranteed Don to throw forth a stream of colourful obscenities and challenges directed at the evolutional retarded and vacant faces of these offenders. Nevertheless apart from the unwitting actions of those who should not be on the water in the first place, we made our way out of the harbour and were soon turning off the engine and setting the sails.

We were now out of the harbour's safety and had passed through the mouth and onto the North Atlantic Ocean. With no small level of apprehension I noted there were few other vessels out in the bay in this weather but I put my faith in Don and did not mention my observation. Don instructed me to take the tiller and gave me a course to follow on the compass. This is not as easy as it sounds, a boat will not travel in a straight line on the water. The action of the wind, waves and tide strive to send the boat in all directions. Some wannabe sailors have difficulties comprehending this fact and one such individual will be mentioned later. As for myself, I clung onto the tiller with one hand while the other clung tightly onto the side of the boat and my eyes remained glued to the compass as the craft rocked and bounced through the water.

As we sailed further out so the waves began to build and the wind howled its fury at the two sailors, or one and a half sailors I should say, daring to venture out on the water in such conditions. Suddenly I realised that the expected six foot swell had grown somewhat larger, huge in fact and as the boat slid down into each trough, all I could see around me was a wall of water. It was frightening to look up and see the waves towering over the boat and I quickly altered my initial impression of the Contessa being a good sized boat. There is nothing like the raging sea to adjust one's impression of size and capabilities, the Contessa had become very small indeed.

Between wondering if I could reach the heads without any biological accidents, I searched for the figure of Don, hoping for some reassurance. It did not help; there he was, stood on top of the cabin section calmly stoking his pipe. He was not hanging onto everything within reach as I was. There he stood like a pillar of granite in defiance of the rolling boat beneath him and the gusting wind about him. I wished I had his confidence but secretly I began to ponder on the state of his sanity. I was terrified, with each wave I bounced on the seat beside the tiller. Slamming down onto my butt and sinking into myself as we hit the bottom of each trough and then being lifted from my seat each time we topped a crest. Only to slam down again! The Contessa constantly changed its position from sailing in a valley of water, surrounded by a liquid wall, to being perched atop a wave made mountain. One moment my vision was obscured by water, the next I could see for miles as the waves lifted the boat high into the air, least I could if the sky was clear. Now the grey heavy skies merged with the grey rolling sea and Don's grey pipe smoke and under this grey blanket the horizon had disappeared. I think the weather forecaster had made a mistake today, strange as that may be. Even for a British summer this weather was grim, and I was sat on the ocean in a tiny boat being pounded by towering waves and a furious wind.

My butt was getting such a pounding as I was continually lifted or slammed onto the hard surface of my seat. It reminded me of my school days. Days before the non-hitting, spanking, battering or the general assault of rebellious small children became taboo in our modern world. My knuckles were white as I gripped the tiller in terror. My hair now lay plastered to my head as the spray from the waves lashed the boat, stinging my face and hands into a lovely shade of frozen red. Did I mention that the temperature had dropped and I was slowly freezing to death in the cockpit of the insignificant Contessa? No? Well it had grown very cold and seemed to be getting even colder. What the heck was I doing here, sailing on telly always seemed to be in warm sunshine but here I was with a sore butt and frozen limbs. Not really my idea of fun!

By now the waves appeared to reach a height of twelve foot or more, not a size to worry an experienced offshore sailor but I was petrified. The wind had begun to howl like a banker forced to give a charitable contribution, the sky grew darker and the spray from the waves thrashing against the hull resembled frozen needles fired from a gun. I was so scared I worried about a spontaneous bowel movement, until I realised my buttocks were clenched so tightly, not even a squeak could escape. I decided I had had enough and looked up to shout to Don that we should get the heck out of here. To my surprise and horror I saw Don quickly tying reefs into the mainsail and even more frightening was the fact that he had attached himself to a safety line, now clipped onto the stainless steel handrails that encircled the sides of the Contessa. Seeing my open mouth and wide eyes, Don signalled that I should turn for shore and head back in. Quickly I peered around searching for sight of the harbour; there was none, only the grey sea. Even when the boat climbed a wave crest I could not see through the gloom that surrounded the Contessa, I was lost in a grey world. What the heck was I going to do now, how would I find the way home? Through the fear and cold my brain snapped into light bulb mode and the solution forced its way to the surface of my befuddled and scared head. Glancing down at the compass I noted our present course and decided to simply reverse it. Turning the boat round, taking care not to be hit by a broaching wave, I set our heading back the way we had come. I rationalised that if our heading had been for instance, 150 degrees south, if I set the compass heading at 330 degrees north, it should take us back to within sight of land and the harbour. Least I really, really hoped so as I could not seek advice from Don for he was busy shortening the sails and trying to keep his pipe alight, he could not have heard me above the wind anyway.

By now I was very scared, what would I do if the pipe smoking apparition fumbling with the sails accidently fell overboard, would I be able to loosen the sails, start the engine and initiate a search for him? How do I start the engine? Don had rushed over that minor point. Would I be able to reach the marine radio and shout for help? Where the heck was the radio anyway? I remember Don stating he had one but for the life of me I could not remember where he said it was. But by far my main concern was my ebbing courage, would I try to find Don in the stormy ocean or would I put my own life first and get to shore in all possible haste. I prayed I would not have to make that decision, because I did not know the answer.

All I could do was keep my hand firmly on the tiller and my attention on the compass, not daring to look up at the raging sea as it strove to send me kicking and gulping into Davey Jones Locker. Suddenly a shape appeared beside me in the cockpit, a sight that very nearly finished off my already twitching bowls. It was Don of course; he had given up trying to reef the mainsail and had lowered it instead. Now only the shortened jib remained to face the wind. With a light but forceful push, Don moved me aside and reached down for the engine starter and a moment later the very welcome sound of mechanical horse power throbbed through the deck. Later Don explained that he had left the jib up in order that the boat would maintain steerage, without at least some sail, manoeuvring the Contessa in such conditions would be difficult. The jib would help keep the vessel facing into the wind and not turning into a broach position until the engine gathered its strength and took over control. I had not noticed Don removing the mainsail but in truth I was not surprised. I kept my gaze away from those grey walls around us and in a desperate bid not to return home as a wet ghost, I focused solely on the compass bearing. I found it also help me to retain my breakfast as the boat heaved and rocked on the deep ocean.

Don then loosened the jib and took over the helm, watching him, I noted with a small degree of pleasure that he remained on the course heading I had chosen; perhaps I was not such an idiot after all. No, belay that comment, only an idiot would be out here on a day like this. If I ever get hold of that weather man I will see how he enjoys having his butt pounded continuously on a hard fibre glass seat! Maybe not, I suspect that comment may give some strange and dark connotations in meaning. My fear began to subside slightly now I had the reassuring company of Don beside me, it did not subside that much though because if he fell in the sea now it would mean I would very likely fall in with him. Dammit! I contemplated using my mobile phone and calling the wife with instructions to place a toilet roll in the fridge. I sincerely considered

I would require much use of the smallest room when and if I finally did get home.

The weather continued to rage around our small vessel and Don struggled to maintain the heading. Mountains of water still climbed high around us before throwing the boat down into the depths of the sea with each cresting and trough of the waves. The crests of grey green angry water played with our boat like a cat plays with a mouse, flinging mermaids, redundant deep sea divers and of course the occasional surfer about its surface with abundant glee. The troughs sent the Contessa down into the bowls of the ocean, allowing glimpses of some bloke with a long wet beard and a trident prodding our hull. I considered using the heads and getting revenge for the screaming sea by dumping something on his head!

But at last the dark shape of land reared in front of us and we could see the gap through which the harbour lay, safety was in sight. Don remained at the helm until we had entered the harbour and the world suddenly become calmer and acceptable once more. The sound of the howling wind died and the water returned to choppy rather than mountainous. The relative peace of the harbour settled on us, or me at least, like a blanket over a comfortable bed and I breathed a sigh of relief before cautiously relaxing my now cramped buttock cheeks. Our adventure over, Don handed me the tiller again while he set about tying and stowing the sails, putting out fenders and all the other chores that follow a sailing trip. I steered slowly and thankfully through the harbour, on past the two bends that I hated so much and back up river to find Don's berth.

Although we had chatted together whenever the ocean allowed us, Don now felt the need to explain.

'Well,' he began, 'that was unexpected. Those were not six foot swells and that was not a force six wind! Whatever the shipping forecast stated, I think they may have gotten it a tad wrong.'

'A tad wrong! I should say so! I admit I was scared witless.'

'Yeah I'm sorry. I didn't mean for your first trip on my new boat to be so troublesome. Next time we'll make sure the weather is fine before we take her out I promise,' muttered Don with a dejected expression on his wind blown face.

'Its fine,' I reassured him, 'at least we know the boat can take it, and it was a good experience for me.

One I would rather not experience again but we can't control the weather.'

'No it was my fault really,' replied Don sheepishly, 'a crew of up to six is recommended for this sized boat. I should not have taken the risk with just you and me aboard. Next time we'll take Ted and one or two others with us, just to be sure.'

Oh great I thought, Don had known he needed more crew but decided to go anyway. But my thoughts were not ungracious; I knew Don had wanted to give me some experience of sailing a larger vessel than I had done so far. And of course he could not have known the forecast would be so wildly inaccurate. So I thanked him anyway and told him I would happily sail with him again, and in fact I did, many times. Though never again in such terrible conditions, I am pleased to say.

I feel I must mention at this point that sailing is an extremely pleasurable pastime, I have recounted some disasters but in truth these are few and far between. It would be boring if I only told tales of sailing on calm waters and under blue skies. The vast majority of my sailing trips were indeed achieved in fine conditions, strongly outweighing the infrequent horrid or frightening ones. I have many memories of sailing gently in a warm breeze with the water lapping a melody upon the hull and the seagulls flying high above me. I recall leisurely trips with my son catching mackerel as we sailed in peace across the bay. Sometimes the sun beat down on me so hot I could not believe I was sailing off the coast of Great Britain, the conditions felt similar to the Mediterranean to me, though I have never been there. There were days when we anchored the Lundy Mist just off a secluded beach where I sat sipping a beer while my son and his friends swam the short distance to shore to explore. I even remember the rare pleasant day out on the water with my wife. Nothing unusual there you may say, but my wife dislikes boats, actually she dislikes any boat larger than a dingy strangely enough. Personally the bigger the boat the safer I feel. She felt the opposite, stating that we could not go far from shore in a dingy. A valid point I suppose. So although I had many relaxing and stress free voyages on Lundy Mist, one can only read about calm seas, blue skies and catching mackerel for so long before one grows bored. So most of the tales I recall will be in a more thrilling and humorous ilk I hope.

So I will continue with another experience in sailing that did not turn out as expected. By now I was a regular in the local boating community and I had made numerous friends along the way. I still considered myself an inexperienced sailor but I was learning. Many of my new friends had yachts and always needed the extra crew member or simply company on a day out. So I often spent more time sailing on someone else's boat than I spent on Lundy Mist. I was grateful to all who offered to take me sailing and in the main I enjoyed each trip. Occasional I learnt something that actually stayed in my brain, always a pleasure. I was lucky not to have experienced the joy of sea sickness during those times, neither had my son who now accompanied me as often as possible. He was keen to learn and enjoyed all aspects of marine activities and it was this keen interest that lead to us both being invited out on for our first trip on a catamaran.

Will was a friend I had met in the local pub which over looked the river and served as a meeting place for all nautical types. He was retired so work was not an interruption to his hobby of sailing. A tall and large thick set man with glasses, a mass of unruly curly greying hair, a round red face and a stomach that could hold numerous pints of assorted beverages. He spoke with a cultured accent which gave an insight into his intellect and was known for his amiability. We became firm friends over the years succeeding our sailing ventures and as he lived quite close to me, we would often share a cup of tea and mull over what boats we would like or where we had sailed. So when he offered to take my son and me out for a sailing trip, his offer was immediately accepted.

On the day of the proposed trip, my son James and I met Will at the quay and used my tender to traverse the short journey out to his large catamaran. I had never been on a catamaran before and was keen for the experience. Once aboard he undertook the obligatory tour, pointing out new gadgets or items of interest. When we came to the engines, I was in for a surprise. Will informed me there were two inboard engines, one in each of the hulls and linked together so they ran in unison but could be used separately. But the surprise came when he told me what the engines were. Petrol engines that were built by the car manufacturer Ford, in fact Will told me, they were the same engines as used in the old Ford Escort. A car made popular first in the early seventies and produced between the years

1968 up until 2002. I had even owned a couple but as for using them to power a thirty foot catamaran, this I was not so sure of. Especially as I had managed to blow up one of my old Ford Escorts in the past, in the middle of nowhere which is often the perfect place for a vehicle to break down. In later years I was to learn that several types of vessel used this same Ford engine as a source of power, but I remained sceptical. However motor car engines in a boat aside, I was still keen to discover how a catamaran sailed. I had always understood this was a very safe design, a catamaran was very difficult to over turn, always a handy property when in the hands of a novice and his son.

Off we set on that morning, heading down river to the harbour, or so we thought. But Will had other ideas. Once away from all the moorings in a wide section of the river and still under engine power, Will suddenly handed the wheel to James and told him to take over. Now poor James was only nine or ten at the time and had never steered a boat in his young life, he had not even steered my little dinghy so piloting a catamaran was terrifying. I stepped up to help him but Will insisted we were safe enough and what better time to try his hand at the wheel. I relented but remained close; I still retained fresh memories of my early sailing trips and knew that boats often decide which way they are going, not the poor soul at the tiller or wheel.

Suddenly Will turned into Captain Bligh. First he had allowed James to head too near to the shore before screaming at him to turn. Of course this caused panic and concern in young James and he forgot which way he was steering and actually turned nearer to the shoreline. I quickly stepped in and spun the wheel in the other direction. I then firmly reminded Will that James was only a young boy and not a professional sailor. Will tried again to get James to steer the boat but the damage was done and James decline with a shake of his head. I think Will then realised he had overstepped the mark and quickly apologised and took over the helm himself.

By mutual agreement we decided to head out to sea where there was more room, hundreds of virtually empty square miles in which both myself and James could have a go at controlling the catamaran in relative safety. Down river we motored and soon reached the harbour and the gate way to the ocean. The day was calm but grey; I concluded a grey sky must be compulsory for sailing lessons, I only hoped the sea would behave itself. It did and the water lay like a silvery grey blanket, albeit with a few creases from a restless night. Out we motored, Will had declared his intention not to raise the sails as it would only complicate matters and he wished to aid us in our quest to handle the boat without the threat of collision and more importantly scratching the shiny paint on his gleaming boat. At first both James and I agreed with this idea, but not for long.

On the water sail boats tend only to rock forwards and back as they crest the waves, the sails and keel stopping them from rolling side to side too much. Motor boats tend to roll side to side like a bow legged sailor on shore with a belly full of rum. They also rock back and forth as they too crest the waves but this is expected. The motion of a smaller motor boat can cause sea sickness amongst those with weak or the morning after stomachs, but most sail with no sudden urges to pebble dash the water's surface. I had never been sea sick before, nor had James to my knowledge. However, on a catamaran with no sails raised and being powered slowly through the water by a single Ford Escort engine soon altered our condition. Will maintained that a slow speed would give James time to steer the boat with no concerns if he chose the wrong way. It was true. James steered happily until he turned a fetching shade of green. A colour that now matched mine for I too was feeling the effects of sea sickness raising from the pit of my stomach and threatening to flow, overboard hopefully. James relinquished the helm and moved off to sit quietly on one of the pair of bows, his feet dangling over the side along with his head, just in case the effects of the sea sickness over powered his digestive system. As for myself, I was hanging over the side of the cockpit, wondering why such a sickness had blighted what should have been a new and interesting experience on a catamaran. Will of course thought it all a great joke as he continued to move over the water slowly, allowing the motion of the sea to control the actions of his vessel.

Between urges I realised what the problem was, it was the shape and design of the catamaran. With twin hulls it bobbed on the water like a square piece of wood, forwards, backwards, port side, starboard side, forward, port side, even corner to corner and backwards with no rhythm or consideration for our sloshing stomachs. Single hulled boats move accordingly to their power source, either sails or the infernal combustion engine. The normal shaped hulls giving either a side ways motion or a see-saw back and forth action. A catamaran moves all over the damn place and it was this action that resulted in James and I imitating aliens, green ones that is. Enough is enough and I looked up at Will and told him to get some speed going. At first he was reluctant, he was enjoying the slow cruise, however I believe the expression on my face warned him otherwise, that and the fact that I threatened to lean into the boat instead of leaning overboard. Any resulting biological action that then occurred would leave his shinning white cockpit splashed with many colours. Mostly orange I suspect, those carrots always appear at times such as this, even if one cannot remember actually eating the damn things.

Will finally obliged and the effects were miraculous. As the vessel built up speed, so the movement changed. From moving about randomly on the waters surface, at last we returned to a familiar movement of forward and back. Both James and I could handle this form of motion and our faces gradually faded from green to grey and then to healthy pink once more. Will was no fool and he realised and acknowledged the change in our features. Keeping the speed of his vessel sufficient to avoid excess motion, he aimed the boat back towards the harbour, wisely deciding we had done enough for that day. By the time we entered the harbour, James and I were fully recovered. James had quickly returned to normal and was even hinting that he was hungry. The constitution of young boys never fails to amaze me, even though at one point, many years ago, I was a boy myself. Yes, surprising is it not? So that was our first and last trip out on a catamaran, I have certainly never been on one since though I cannot say for sure that James has not since he has become a man, but some how I doubt it.

I sailed frequently both on my own Lundy Mist and with Don and any other obliging idiot that would risk allowing this Jonah on board their vessel. Except for Will's catamaran of course, I never really felt the desire to experience that again. The hobby of sailing had truly entered my soul by now and I eagerly accepted any opportunity to ride the waves. However it soon became difficult to find a crew to accompany me on Lundy Mist as commitments gradually ate away at the small band of sailors willing to assist me. I could sail reasonably well by now however I never did gain the self confidence required to sail off into the sunset completely alone. I realised I would never emulate Sir Francis Chichester or my modern day hero, Ellen MacArthur in a sailing vessel. It was time for a change I decided, and so after several years of sailing, I made the momentous decision try my hand at the mechanical variety of marine craft.

Chapter Eight: Spots before my eyes.

We had owned the Lundy Mist for several years and I learnt more and more about the art of sailing, but let's be honest, sailing was not to be my forte. Each summer I sailed as much as possible, my friends rallying round in an attempt to help teach this retarded mariner. Unfortunately time moves on and it was with a great sadness that I decided to sell the Lundy Mist and seek out a new vessel that did not depend on wind for propulsion. I was not a confident sailor and even I knew it would not be long before I drowned someone or more likely my own stupid self.

However I was to discover that selling a boat is not as easy as one might think. Placing advertisements in the appropriate media is no arduous task, though I never considered how expensive it would be. Nor did I contemplate the type of person that would answer my advertisement, I naturally assumed only those with a genuine interest in my boat would reply. My conclusion was wrong, for every genuine sailor that came to check over the Lundy Mist, so I had dozens of wannabe fishermen who wanted a boat but had idea what type other than something to chuck out a fishing line over the side. I also had hordes of gentlemen who thought they could achieve a bargain by feigning disinterest and offering a stupidly low figure. I was still very fond of the Lundy Mist and I was not about to sell it cheap to someone who only wanted to catch mackerel. Soon I began to despair and almost gave up trying to sell my boat. I would rather keep it and look after it than give ownership over to someone who would not give it the care that it required. In truth I did not really mind keeping the vessel, I had obviously grown quite attached to it and it was only the anticipation of purchasing a new toy that kept me going.

I slowed all my efforts to sell my boat and continued to have fun, mishaps and adventures on it while still keeping an eye open for the unwary purchaser. My wife whose name is Joy, a slight contradiction in terms but I am keeping quiet, and my daughter June did not care what boat I owned, neither were keen on boating to say the least. The few times I did manage to persuade them on board usually ended in some minor disaster or another. The infamous Seagull outboard accounted for a few of these mishaps. I believe the damn thing knew my wife and daughter

139

were not such eager sailors as we two family males. On numerous occasions the thing gave up on us in the middle of the river, I was not allowed to take them out to sea. My life is important to me and it would not be worth living if I even suggested a trip out of the harbour.

When on board as a family unit and under strict instructions from the female members, we simply stayed on the river and made use of the local events and attractions that frequented our small piece of the world. On one particular day we had planned to sail, correction - motor down river to take part in an annual festival that celebrated the marine heritage of the small harbour. Amongst all the activities a torchlight procession by boat was due to be held and we all agreed to take part. I purchased the recommended torches, basically thick sticks with one end covered in a combustible material, reminiscent of medieval flame torches, and armed with a packed supper, off we set. Night was falling as we neared the harbour, a useful time of day for a torchlight procession, sunlight would have damped the event I concluded. It would not be much of a procession if one cannot see the lit torches. Joy and June remained huddled in the cabin for most of the trip down river, James on the other hand, was thrilled, not only to be out on the river, but to be out on the river at night. I was grateful I had maintained all my navigation lights because I soon joined a multitude of other assorted craft making their way towards the harbour. Later that night I was to learn why the colour of ones boat can be important.

We took our place in the procession and joined the throng of vessels with owners and crews all holding their torches aloft as we motored slowly through the harbour and up to the main quay. It was a spectacular sight; the harbour was aglow with coloured lights strung across lamp posts, guttering and anyone who remained standing inactive for too long. The visiting yachts, at the sound of a horn, all switched on whatever lights their vessel possessed, navigation lights, cabin lights and hand torches all gleamed in the darkness of night. We too held our torches high, myself and James now joined by my wife and daughter, four more torches to add to the snake like procession of light that floated on the water. The evening passed delightfully, my wife had brought hot soup and sandwiches which we munched happily while watching all the spectacular scenes about us, both on the water and onshore.

Finally at around ten thirty all the fireworks and festivities concluded and we began the trip up river and home. I had equipped us with a selection of torches as even my limited knowledge and inadequate brain had realised it would be pitch dark on the return journey. It has to go down as one of my few wise moments in my life. The river was indeed very dark, though we could make out the differences between water, land and sky. We did not require the torches as we motored contentedly under a starlit sky, however finding our moorings presented a challenge I had not foreseen. I think I mentioned earlier that I had chosen to paint my little tender a nice shade of blue, not a dark blue in must be said, but a blue with a dark enough hue that it could not been seen in the dark!

We reached the area where we were berthed but could not see a thing. A small blue boat bobbing on the water amongst all the other dark shapes was invisible. Slowly I motored on with James on the bow with a torch and Joy on one side and June on the other, both also armed with torches. I had my navigation lights on but they are there so others could see me, not so I could see around me. We continued on, I was heading for the general area in which I hoped to glimpse my dinghy and not run into any of the other moored vessels in my way. Other craft were also returning to their berths but they had the intelligence to paint their boats white and appeared to have little trouble compared to us. Obviously a white boat will show up clearly in torchlight, but a blue one does not. At last a cry from James announced he had discovered our elusive tender, he had used his brain and searched for the large white yacht that held the berth adjacent to mine. Once he had found that, I knew I would find my berth on the far side of it, least that is what I hoped.

Finally there was our tiny boat, a dark shadow on the water and only just visible in James torchlight. I slowed the engine even further until we were barely crawling along and gently steered towards our dinghy. James already had the boat hook in hand and snagged up the pick up line as I edged near. Finally we were home, well we were moored at least, next came the closing down of Lundy Mist and a row across the river still in complete darkness. Happily a small boat powered by oars will not make a large dent in anything I might inadvertently crash into, but still everyone kept a sharp lookout for me and I directed our boat back to its shore berth with no mishaps. Satisfied after a lovely evening, disregarding the bit about not finding our dinghy, we piled into the nearby pub for a fortifying nightcap, or three.

The next morning I returned to the Lundy Mist to make sure I had not forgotten anything the night before. I was relieved to see it swinging happily on its mooring. At least I had tied it up securely. Once on board I looked around for any jobs I had not done and to make sure the engine was shut down properly. I was working away in contentment when I noticed something strange. As I looked around I saw the Lundy Mist was splattered with spots of a bright green substance. Now I thought, if that is seagull droppings, then there is a bird flying about with a serious problem. Taking my life into my hands, and nose, I examined the stuff closer; it was wax, green wax! Suddenly I realised what all the mess was, candle wax from the flaming torches we used the night before during the local river procession and celebration. I felt a slight annoyance with James but it did not last. He was not to know that as he scampered over the boat to peer at items of interest during the festival, so he had trailed wax over almost every surface of the boat. No matter how the green spots got there, it was now up to me to remove

144

them. Using a paint scrapper left onboard following a recent repaint and spruce up of the Lundy Mist, I gently began prying off the wax. It took me a couple of hours to find and remove all the bright green wax. I filled a bucket with a cleaning fluid mixed with river water and set to cleaning off the stains. Guess what? Yep the damn stains would not shift, they refused to budge one little bit and I was left with a green spotty deck that would certainly attract numerous odd comments from my fellow boating friends. Sure enough at that very moment the first one drew alongside in his dinghy, armed with the obligatory cans of beer. In surprise I checked my watch and only then realised noon had come and gone. I had not realised the removal of the wax blobs had taken as long so I felt justified in accepting one of the cans.

'Gone for a new colour scheme?' asked Steve with a grin, 'I see you took part in the torchlight thing then?'

'Yep!'

'Well you know them wax stains won't come out, don't you?' commented Steve as he clambered onboard.

'Yeah I've just discovered that. What the heck do they put in those candle torch thingies anyway? If the wax can stain paintwork like this, the dye used in the green colour must be very potent. Looks like I'm going to repaint the damn boat again, perhaps I should send the bill to the Harbour office. What do you think?'

'Hahaha, well you can try but I wouldn't advise it. You go upsetting the old harbour master and you'll end up regretting it. Crusty old bugger he is, good at his job but you don't want to go arguing with him. Just paint the damn boat and stop moaning. Anyway it could do with brightening up a bit.'

Concluding his opinion, Steve made himself comfortable on the cockpit seat and pulled the ring tab from his beer can.

'Brighten it up? I've only just finished repainting it, how can it need brightening up? The paint on it is barely a month old!'

'There you go then,' grinned Steve, 'been there a month, needs brightening now.'

'Shut up Steve!'

'Huh, that's a nice thing to say to someone just offering a bit of advice, but as a matter of interest, what colour you going to paint it this time?' replied Steve with a theatrical down cast expression.

'What do you mean, what colour?'

'Well I don't like this spotty stuff you got on here, maybe plain white would better suit?'

'Shut up Steve!'

So the very next fine day, I had to wait several days, this is Britain after all. I set off armed with a flask of tea and a packed lunch to catch the outgoing tide. I planned to stay on the Lundy Mist until the chore was completed so hopefully by the time I finished, the tide would be coming back in and I would be able to get back to shore again. I had purchased more white paint for the deck and superstructure along with more anti-slip paint. I wanted the boat gleaming in case some one took up my 'for sale' offer and wished to see the Lundy Mist in all its glory. Once on board I set about cleaning the decks again, numerous little gifts left by the seagulls joined with the green spots to give the vessel a slightly psychedelic appearance that tamed any appetite I may have had.

The sun shone down on me as I worked in the peace and quiet of the river, the tide finally left me and

I was marooned on the river bed, supported by the two bilge keels that stood like thick legs beneath the hull and balanced by the sturdy rudder. Standing firmly on the sandy bottom made the chore of painting much easier, trying to hold a paint brush steady while the tide and water kept the boat in constant motion can be a challenge. My local river was, as I have mentioned before, actually an estuary and therefore is strongly influenced by the tides. By choosing a period of spring tides and catching the few hours between the water going out and coming in made my day slightly easier. I must admit that it was the weather that forced my decision to paint that day, it was simply pure luck that the tides matched my chores, and not any expert planning on my behalf.

Seagulls flew about me and birds chattered in the trees on the shore, the sun shone and the weather was warm, it was a perfect day to be on board a boat in the middle of a dry river. One would think that and I did, at first. It was not long before I discovered how difficult it can be to apply a bright coat of white paint under the full glare of the sun. I soon wished I had either brought along a pair of sunglasses or I had thrown those damn wax torches over board in the first place. However I continued, streaming and aching eyes battling against the relentless dazzle that beamed down from the sun and reflected right back up into my face. If I missed any areas on the deck it would just be too bad, I could not have cared less by that point. The white paint acted like snow. Though how I was going to explain to anyone I had managed to get snow blindness I could not say. I was very relieved when all the white was completed and it was time to redo the anti-slip patches on the bow, decks and cabin roof. This colour was a pale blue, a light colour but not light enough to blind me and after several minutes I realised I could see clearly once more.

At last all the painting was completed and the tide had returned to enough depth to allow me to climb into the tender and row back to shore. I cleared away all the paint, the bushes and the now empty flask and lunch box. I had in the main part enjoyed my day of solitude on board the Lundy Mist in the tranquil setting of the river, but now it was time to head home. I fervently hoped the seagulls would have the decency to wait until the paint dried before alighting on my vessel again, but I was not going to hold my breath. It was a risk I had to take, thoughts of holding a loaded shotgun with a crapping seagull in my sights was my greatest wish at that time. Most of the paint had now dried to the tacky stage so it would not be long before it would withstand webbed feet, feathers and digested food waste. I had purposely begun the day by painting the bow first because that is where most of the seagull activity took place. Next to be repainted was the cabin roof and finally the decks and walkways. It was a brilliant idea at the start of the day, but not such a bright idea now.

I suddenly realised by painting the decks last, I was effectively trapped! How the heck was I going to climb over the sides to get aboard my tender when all the paint was still considerably wet? This was the last straw and I began to rant and rave. Damn seagulls, damn green wax, damn wet paint and damn stupidity! Looking around the gleaming Lundy Mist all I saw was fresh wet paint everywhere, filling my eyes with its brilliance. The other thing I noticed were a group of seagulls flying high above me while uttering what to my ears sounded like laughter at my self induced plight. How the heck was I going to get off my boat without getting myself covered in paint and destroying my entire days work? My cursing continued.

I had painted the entire deck and anything in reach of a seagull's bottom or splattered with green wax. I had even painted areas that did not really require another coat, I had been thorough to the tenth degree and now I was stuck. The only thing on the superstructure I had not painted was the engine. Hang on a minute I thought, I had not painted the engine or the small area around the engine area. The outboard motor was secured to the transom on an outboard motor bracket, the most common way of attaching a smaller outboard engine to the stern of a sailing boat with a rudder. Mine was no different except that beneath the clamps I had fitted a stainless steel plate on that section of the inner transom in order to avoid causing any damage to the wooden transom. It was this plate I had not painted and so it was this plate that might allow me to escape the painted prison on which I stood.

I could only see one problem concerning this avenue of escape; I was definitely not a contortionist. Basically I would have to pull the tender close to the stern, climb over the Mercury engine and some how get down into the tender without falling into the now full flowing river. I decided to go for it, what did I have to lose apart from spoiling all my hard work, and a drowning of course. I leaned out over the stern and grasped the rope that held the tender attached to the Lundy Mist, making sure I did not touch any of the wet paint. Pulling it as tight as I could up against the motor I prayed that the propeller would not pierce the plywood hull of the small dinghy, it was my life line to the shore and more importantly, my evening meal. The shaft and propeller of the Mercury engine were propped via its bracket at an angle of about forty five degrees out of the water, a normal practice when leaving an engine attached to the stern when not in use or at moorings. Next I stood carefully on the unpainted stern seat and gently stretched one leg out over the engine. Once astride the Mercury I followed my leg with the rest of my body until I was virtually sat on the engine cover. I prayed the bracket would hold my weight along with that of the engine. I grasped the tender's rope and attempted to position it as close as possible beneath my dangling leg. Finally with a desperate thought for my manhood, I wiggled and slid over the engine and down into the tender bobbing behind the Lundy Mist. Unfortunately as my centre of gravity moved from the stern to the motor, my momentum carried me right over and I landed face down on the floor of the tender with my legs bashing against the rear seat bench.

At last I was safe and without any more mishaps other than bruised shins and a slightly flatter nose. Scrambling upright I looked back at the Lundy Mist and checked I had not forgotten anything before loosening the rope that joined the two craft. Leaving the newly painted vessel swaying gently on its berth, I allowed the tender to drift off on the tide while I straightened myself and prepared to attack the oars and head back to shore. I was feeling very pleased with myself for the job done and the minor fact that I was still in one piece and, I was dry. With a satisfied sigh I reached out my hands to place them on the oars and noticed something strange on my right hand. Looking closer I saw my entire palm and fingers were covered in white paint. Some how I had managed to lay my hand on the wet paint and now there were white hand prints all over the floor and seat of the tender. Peering back at the Lundy Mist, I could now see one prominent hand print visible on the stern of the Lundy Mist. My thoughts at that moment cannot be repeated.

Several days later and following my attempt at imitating Picasso, a gent called and stated he was interested in purchasing the Lundy Mist. We agreed a time and arranged to meet in the river side pub. I was now feeling very reluctant to sell the Lundy Mist but reason stated I should. I was not a competent sailor and it had become even harder to find a willing and experienced sailor to accompany me. Minor inconveniences like work, family commitments and a strong desire to survive meant finding volunteers whose spare time coincided with my free time was almost impossible. There was also the fact that my wife still had no desire to undertake any sailing trips or motoring trips for that matter. So I held firm and kept my appointment with the prospective buyer, though even that did not turn out as expected.

On the agreed day I made my way down to the river but harboured extreme doubts concerning the possibility of boarding the Lundy Mist on such a day. The wind was howling and the water was covered in small galloping white horses created by the action of wind over tide. The gent was waiting for me at the pub and I immediately expressed my concern at attempting to cross the river in those conditions. Describing him as an aged Teddy boy from the fifties would be quite accurate, thick black hair, obviously dyed and styled into the infamous DA or *ducks arse* as it was commonly known, with a lined face and a hand rolled cigarette dangling from thin lips. I judged he was of average height and build, what ever the average might be. He was dressed in a thick waterproof coat, old and stained jeans and - dainty highly polished fashionable loafers! My opinion of him being an experienced sailor dropped significantly at the sight of those extremely unsuitable shoes. I find myself constantly shocked by what many people consider suitable foot wear for boating activities. I believe I have already mentioned the heavy woman in stiletto heels threatening to sink my little boat by driving her heels straight through the hull. If I have not then I apologise and will hopefully remember to mention the story later on.

But I digress, I explained to the fifties rock and roller that it would be unwise to be out on the water that day but he insisted, in fact I can still remember his exact words:

'It's only a river, what can happen on a river? It's not the sea so I don't see a problem. Let's get over to your boat so I can have a look around before I decided to buy it or not.'

'Okay, if we must,' I replied, 'however if I decided it is too dangerous we'll turn around and come straight back. Do you agree?'

The old Teddy boy agreed and with much reluctance I launched my tender and started rowing across the half mile stretch to the Lundy Mist bobbing and swaying violently on the restless water. We did make it to the vessel but by now the wind had grown in strength and the water was fast becoming treacherous. I began to panic. On board the Teddy boy was examining every thing he considered important but in truth had no bearing on the seaworthiness of the vessel. A boat will not flounder or sink if the cooker does not work or the toilet flush is out of action, nor will any lives be placed in danger if the bunk cushions are not soft enough. Finally my patience gave out and I stated firmly that I was heading back to shore; he had the choice of accompanying me or swimming back. With a slight snarl he unwillingly agreed and we boarded the tender again, though this time it was made difficult by the increased bucking and rocking of the small craft.

The tide was very strong and I knew I would not be able to row straight across the water to my shoreline mooring. I set off down river in the direction of the tidal stream, virtually letting the boat drift along the tide, much to the surprise of my passenger. I knew the currents would be strong in those conditions and I also knew where they would be the strongest so I went with the flow so to speak, rowing furiously to avoid broaching rather than gain ground. The currents surged along the river but there where a couple of places where these currents slackened and it was to such a spot I steered my little dinghy. As the pull of the river eased I quickly made a right turn and headed across the river at the point of weakest resistance, before finally coming back up on the less violent side of my moorings. Instead of a short straight trip from the Lundy Mist to my frappe, I had been forced to make a huge U turn and travel three times the distance to simply make the same journey across the river. The Teddy boy was now very quiet, his face had turned ashen and the knuckles of his hands were white as he gripped tightly to each side of the very mobile craft.

After a battle, we at last hit the calmer water that reached out some five metres from the shore. Once in that section it was relatively easy to manoeuvre onto the mooring and tie up the tender. Climbing out of the craft we both stood on shore and gave a sigh of relief. I had been scared because even though I thought I knew what to expect, it had actually been much worse. I may have been new to sailing but I had lived in the area for much of my life and had a healthy respect for the water. I clenched my buttocks and portrayed a brave face because the Teddy boy was visibly shaking by now. The fear of what he had just experienced was taking its toll and his hands shook even more as he attempted to roll another cigarette.

'Bloody hell! That was rough, I didn't think we were going to make it!' he exclaimed in between puffs on his cigarette.

'Yeah, it's surprising how rough it can get on our little river!' I retorted as I picked up my oars and began making my way back to the pub, it was time for a drop of something fortifying.

Chapter Nine: Yellow Peril.

As I expected, the Teddy boy did not buy the Lundy Mist, in fact I never heard from him again. I was not surprised. So over the next few weeks I continued to advertise the vessel though only half heartedly. I was worried that the sailing season was fast approaching its conclusion and who the heck would want to buy a sailing sloop in winter. No one would think of marine activities while sheltering from pouring rain, hammering hail, freezing winds and the constant rumour of snow. And that was just our summer, it gets worse in winter! Luckily I was wrong. One evening I received a phone call at home. The caller introduced himself and enquired if I was the owner of the Lundy Mist. I replied that I was and asked the reason for his call. He proceeded to inform me that he had seen my boat on the river and had taken a liking to it. He had tried to catch me on several occasions but had not been successful, so he obtained my phone number from a mutual friend and decided to call. To my surprise he then offered the full asking price for the Lundy Mist. I tried not to jump up and down, drop the phone in shock or allow any glee into my voice as I paused for an instant, I wanted to give the impression that I was actually giving the matter serious thought. Then I quickly accepted. We arranged a time for him to inspect my boat and I went to bed happy that night.

A few days later I watched my once pride and joy sail off down river. The new owner had decided against transporting it by road. Instead he wished to get a feel of the vessel by sailing it round the coast to the next harbour where he intended to keep it. I was sorry to see it go but eager to acquire a new craft in which to continue my nautical lessons, and of course, play with a new toy. Neither John nor my wife Joy were particularly happy with my decision, John I could understand but why my wife cared I had no idea. She did not like boats anyway. So it was purely down to me and James. He was equally eager to discover a new experience on the water and initiate the search for a new vessel. He had quickly gotten over the fear of sea sickness and it had not bothered either of us since that floating square board known as a catamaran. James had recently accompanied Don and me out on the Contessa a few times without any qualms, though not when we were racing. So the hunt began for a new boat, but first there was some more unexpected fun.

While seeking another craft I managed to come into ownership of a ten foot bright yellow inflatable boat. It was a strange sort of craft, a half hexagon bow and the same shape at the stern with long straight sides. A bracket was attached at the stern to enable the fitting of an outboard engine and slated floorboards helped one remain upright in the boat. Believe me, without the floor boards it would have been like trying to walk in a bouncy castle. In size it was ten foot or three metres long and approximately five foot across the beam. Two inflatable tubes crossed its width, serving as seats or life buoys if required, though hopefully not. The whole set up was accompanied by two short oars with wooden handles and plastic blades. Pretty useless really but they came with the boat so who was I to argue? I cannot in truth remember how I got it, but it certainly gave us much entertainment. As I said I cannot remember how I acquired the yellow inflatable nor can I remember what make it was. I know it was not an Avon or a Capri so I should have known better, but alas I did not. Both James and I were keen to try out this floating banana and at the earliest opportunity we manhandled in into my van and set off for the river. I took along the old Seagull as the Mercury had gone with the Lundy Mist. At the quay side we took turns in inflating the thing via its own foot pump, a task that took much longer than I expected and I was soon to discover the reason why.

Finally the yellow monster was firmly inflated and eagerly we launched it onto the water and climbed in. Being a rather large inflatable, we did not expect it to sink, but after only a few moments on the water, sink is what it began to do. Luckily we were only a matter of yards from shore so following some furious paddling with the two plastic oars, we quickly reached safety. Scrambling back on land, James and I dragged the now seriously deflated lump of rubber onto the slipway and inspected our latest acquisition in disgust. We finally deduced it was leaking like a sieve though we could see no visible sign of air escaping, but what other reason could it be. Pumping it up again we watched closely to see what happened, we saw nothing but still the air escaped like a silent fart. Neither of us was keen to try it out on the water again so we removed what little air remained in the yellow peril and stuffed it back into my van before heading home in disappointment.

Not knowing what to do about the deflated inflatable, I rang round several specialists and discovered one not six miles from me. Speaking to the owner I asked if he could fix the thing and was assured that he could. So the next day I bundled the inflatable into my van and set off to get the yellow peril fixed. Once there and upon closer inspection, the specialist informed me that the inflatable had become porous, a fact I had not what I expected to hear. Who ever heard of a porous rubber inflatable dinghy? Weird! It's certainly not a good idea to have pores in something supposed to be airtight, watertight and float. He said he could fix it by pumping it full of a rubber sealant which would in theory create a second skin on the interior of the craft and thus seal all the minute leaks. I considered this idea to be somewhat foolish but agreed to pay the price for the repairs. Within a week I received the call to say my yellow peril was resealed and ready to go, so off I set with the pleasurable company of my wife alongside me in my van, to reclaim the now hopefully leak proofed craft.

At the time I was still running my own business and I owned an old Ford Transit van that doubled as the family car. Upon the van was a sturdy roof rack and it was upon this that I intended transporting the fully inflated dinghy home. The specialist had warned me not to deflate it for a few weeks in order to allow the sealant to set properly. An hour later with the bill paid, the yellow peril was attached to the roof rack by means of those stretchy bungee strap things that tend to be used more often than string or rope these days.

All went well and Joy and I headed home. I was busy driving and wondering where I was going to store the thing as the specialist had instructed me not to leave it in direct sun light. My shed was certainly not big enough and I doubted the wife would let me keep it in our bedroom or behind the telly in the living room. Strange I know but that's what wives are like, no consideration for the needs of impractical husbands. I had just concluded that it would go in the back garden and I would cover it with a tarpaulin when Joy suddenly gave a shout.

'Stop!' she cried.

Quickly I pulled the van over to the side of the road, glancing quickly in my mirror to check no alien spacecraft or over zealous policeman was sneaking up behind me. Next I checked all the dials on the dashboard in case something was wrong with the engine. Finally I looked over at the wife and with raised eyebrows asked the reason for her shout.

'Look!' she cried, 'look behind us. No not on the road. Look up in the air!'

She's finally lost the plot I thought as I lifted my gaze to the sky behind our parked van. Then I received a shock. There against the azure sky was a strange flying object, a strange yellow flying object! The inflatable dinghy had broken loose from its restraints and was now soaring up into the air some thirty foot above the road. Picture the scene. There I was, staring open mouthed out of my van window at a huge rubber kite. The wind swirled on top of the hill, aided by the fact that it was a junction, a road shooting off to the right allowing more wind to float our boat in the most unexpected way. Higher and higher flew the yellow boat, surprising the heck out of the birds roosting in the tree tops. As I watched in horror, a lull in the gusts allowed the wind to halt its frantic attempts to place the first ever yellow inflatable boat on the moon and die down just long enough for the craft to float gently back down to earth. The period between gusts did not last long however and within seconds the damn yellow lump of rubber was shooting up into the sky once again. Joy and I dashed from the van, hoping to catch it between gusts and before it took off again or it was squashed by the traffic. This was quite a busy road.

Suddenly I noticed an even stranger sight, an ice cream van had been travelling behind us and the driver had witnessed everything. With quick thinking the ice cream man turned his van across the centre of the road in order to block the oncoming traffic. With the aid of his hazard warning lights and the vans tannoy system blaring out the '*Popeye the Sailor man*' tune appropriately in place of a siren, the road was safely blocked by a brightly painted red, white and blue ice cream vehicle. A ridiculous sight I accept, but it worked and the traffic stopped. Out jumped the driver as he rushed to assist in the capture of the yellow menace. Another drop in the wind and the yellow peril floated down to within our grasp. But not near enough as yet another gust sent it sailing up towards the stratosphere once again. With arms stretched to the sky, Joy, me and the ice cream man ran in frantic circles beneath the yellow kite. Each time the wind dropped the boat floated back down to earth and within inches of our grasp before soaring up again.

I was rapidly running out of breath, stamina and the will to live at this point. My spirit had been broken by an air bound yellow Unidentified Flying Object. By now of course we had quite an audience of fellow drivers, dog walkers and NASA observers gathered about us in the middle of the road. Nice traffic jams were building on each of the three roads that led to the junction but no one appeared to mind, the spectacle before them was just too good to miss. Finally with a mighty leap, the ice cream man managed to get a hold on the flying inflatable and bring it down to within reach of myself and Joy. To a round of applause from the queued drivers and impromptu audience, we wrestled the thing down.

When the craft was secured by my wife actually sitting in it upon the ground, I thanked the ice cream man and waved my gratitude at the queuing traffic. I was concerned I had annoyed those drivers waiting to continue their journey. I need not have worried. The traffic remained stationary for a few more moments while the drivers wiped their eyes and attempted to cease their laughter at the sight of a ten foot yellow boat flying through the air whist chased by me, my wife and an ice cream vendor. Finally the road cleared enough for me and the wife to once more secure the craft to the roof rack of my van. This time I took no chances and tied the damn thing down with rope from the van, this time it was going nowhere. It had certainly been a new experience seeing a large bright yellow boat flying through the air.

Although we now owned a very versatile inflatable craft that could travel over water or through the air, James and I continued our search for another boat, a real boat not a blow up one. We did use the inflatable frequently, it was something of a novelty being able to zoom about the water with no fear of grounding or hitting any other craft. If we had hit something else, the soft rubber construction of the dinghy would act as a bumper, and most likely send us rebounding away like a rubber ball. We regularly used the Seagull which was behaving itself nicely. We both found the oars to be virtually a joke so declined to use them unless absolutely necessary. A rubber boat is surprisingly difficult to row, the wind and tide, passing fish and flatulence will all affect its direction with ease. However the very best thing about the shallow draft of a rubber dinghy was the fact it only needed a bare few inches of water on which to float, unlike other boats and especially yachts and motor cruisers. Speaking of yachts, we did have an amusing episode one afternoon on the river.

James and I were pottering about in the dinghy and had decided to travel up river as far as we could. It was neap tides so the water was not deep and it gradually decreased to just a few inches deep, without going out entirely as it did during the spring tides. We were not concerned about this fact, we were both attired in suitable wellington boots and knew that if we got stuck further up the river, we could simply walk to shore or turn the inflatable around and head back to deeper water. We knew this fact, all the local boatmen knew this fact and even visiting sailors who could read a chart knew this fact. But there is always one, one who does not check his charts or almanac, one who believes he is a brilliant sailor and needs no advice from others. One of these idiots was following James and me now.

Thinking nothing of it at the time, we continued up river in search of new sights and possibly adventures. I could see that the seaweed on the river bottom was just beginning to show its head on the surface of the water. I knew it would not be much further before we ran out of depth. Still I worried not a jot, James watched the Mullet swim up river to snag any tasty morsels caught out by the receding tide. Mullet are not the most favoured fish of the angling fraternity, feeding mostly on detritus and the occasional smaller creatures or substances even more appalling. Mullet could be described as an acquired taste to say the least. However it was still a pleasure to see them scurrying about the river bed and seaweed. Up river we continued, enjoying the calm and tranquil environment of the river with its high hilled banks covered in trees. We watched birds flying and singing, other birds floating and quacking. Kingfishers leapt from overhanging branches and dived for fish in a dash of brilliant colour while Cormorants drifting lazily upon the gently lapping water. Herons stalked the shoreline searching for any stray morsel of food that may unwittingly show itself and high above all a Common Buzzard glided silently over our peaceful scene.

In between day dreams I had kept a wary eye on a yacht coming up some distance to our stern. I gave it no serious consideration as I expected it was simply heading back to its moorings and I assumed the skipper knew what he was doing. The yacht was approximately twenty five to twenty seven foot long and was a sloop of some type. I did not know or care. It was just another boat invading my river as far as I was concerned. I could see four or five people on board and as their voices carried across the calm and still waters I could identify that they were not local. This of course was nothing unusual as tourism played a huge part in the local economy and visitors were a common plague throughout the sailing season. I also detected in those loud voices evidence that possibly alcohol may have been consumed on board. But I remained unconcerned though I felt slightly annoyed that their voices disturbed the peace and quiet of the area. I expected the vessel to turn soon and head off to where ever it was destined; least then it would be quiet once more.

Sudden the river bed scrapped the bottom of our dinghy and I quickly tilted the Seagull out of the water before it became entangled in seaweed, sunken treasure or lost scuba divers. James and I then climbed out of the dinghy in readiness to pull it the short distance back down river to where there was enough water depth for the craft to float. It was then I suddenly heard a crescendo of cries from the yacht behind us. Either the people on board thought they had just

171

witnessed a miracle and James and I were walking on water. Perhaps they had finally realised the water was too shallow for their large vessel. I decided it was probably the latter but one can never be sure. Turning to see what the fuss was about, James and I watched as those onboard the yacht dashed about the vessel in a scene reminiscent of a comedy show as they vainly attempted to halt its progress into the shallow water. Moments later a clunk was clearly heard across the water as the boat came to an abrupt halt, its keels stuck firmly in the muddy river bed. The happy sailors suddenly found themselves marooned in the middle of the river with the tide still falling.

I could not believe anyone could be so stupid, it was now apparent that the skipper of the yacht did not know the river and had decided to follow us. Who in their right mind would follow an inflatable boat with a very shallow draft with a craft that required a depth of several feet in which to float? I muttered a derisory comment while James simply laughed at the self induced plight of the people now stranded mid river. Together we hauled our dinghy the few feet back down river until it floated before climbing back in and rowing towards deeper water. Once we had gained a

Wellington boot depth beneath us, I restarted the Seagull and we began motoring along. As we drew level with the stranded yacht, the person I assumed was the skipper called out for help. I grinned back at him and told him and his companions to settle back and wait, the tide would return in six hours or so. There was not enough room in our rubber boat for all of them so there was little I could do anyway. I called across to him that I would let the harbour office know of his position in case anyone was waiting for their return and worried. However at this offer, the stranded skipper grew rather red in the face and requested I keep this information to myself. He did not wish any further embarrassment than he was suffering at that moment. I agreed and with a cheery wave from both of us, James and I continued on our way.

We had not travelled far when the next batch of visitors or nautical idiots passed us. Flying up river with total disregard for the six knot speed limit imposed on the river, sped a small fishing trawler type vessel about twenty to twenty five foot in length. It was clinker built with a compact wheel house and fishing equipment perched on its stern. On it I could see several young people and I guessed the oldest would be about fourteen. This youth was at the wheel and laughing with another lad and at least two young girls. They ignored our attempts to warn them of shallow waters and one even returned our waves with a rude gesture. Seeing that, both James and I decided to leave them to their own stupidity and we motored on.

I pondered on the mental capability of those parents who would allow such young people to venture out unsupervised in such a vessel. No one I knew would do such a thing, James was certainly never allowed out on our boats by himself, and in truth he had enough sense not to take the risk anyway. It was not long after that the cheerful voices of the youngsters changed into cries of alarm. They had reached the area in which the yacht was marooned when their boat lurched to a halt. Now there were two vessels that would be waiting helplessly throughout the day for the returning tide. I concluded they both obviously needed the lesson and hoped they would learn from it. Deep down I seriously doubted it.

Sadly but not really unexpectedly, over the course of that season, the sealant inside the yellow peril began to fail and once more it lost its ability to float. I considered it might still fly but I was not about to attempt that again. Finally the time came when the yellow inflatable was assigned to Ebay and another unsuspecting owner. We had lots of fun in the thing but the search for a real boat continued. I had never owned a rubber inflatable dinghy before and I have not owned one since. I think the experience of that yellow floating and flying craft cured me of any future desire I might have had in air filled rubber contraptions.

Chapter Ten: Moving on.

The sailing season was drawing to a close before we discovered our new boat. We had used the yellow peril for much of the remaining season and enjoyed the ease and manoeuvrability of the craft. We could obviously not venture out to sea in it but the river provided enough entertainment and items of interest to ensure we made the most of the summer on the water. With the weather growing cold and wet, or should I say wetter, we stored the deflated yellow menace away in the shed until it sold, suitably secured with manacles and chains to avoid any more flying trips by the boat that thought it was a kite. I considered the sailing season over and prepared to stay warm and dry away from the nautical scene for the winter when out of the blue, a friend called and informed me he was selling his boat and would I be interested. I should have been warned because he seemed very keen to sell it on the phone, but I wanted another boat as soon as possible so I took no heed. I decided to take a look at it anyway.

After some thought I concluded that if I did acquire his boat, I would refit and undertake any repairs over winter so it would be ready to use as soon as the British weather stopped trying to drown or freeze us. My friend talked up the brilliance and seaworthiness of his boat. But he would, he wanted to sell the thing. I gathered from his flowery description that his vessel was indeed the type of craft I had been searching for. Discussions between me, my wife, John, my wife, my son James; the wife, June my daughter, and not forgetting the wife Joy, she likes to discuss things fully. I finally agreed to inspect this marvellous vessel with a view to purchasing it.

First impressions can sometimes lead to disappointment and my initial impression and opinion of the craft in question did little to overwhelm me with delight. My prospective new boat, my new toy was safely berthed and covered I was informed, though its exact location was still unknown and for an obvious reason as it turned out. The day of our inspection arrived and James and I had agreed to meet my friend called Jack just outside our little village. We had been warned to bring wellington boots so both James and I assumed the boat would be in or at least near water; hence the need for boots. We met up with Jack and following the obligatory greetings, we followed him in our car as he lead the way to the mysterious craft in his own vehicle. It did not take but a few moments to realise we were not heading in the direction of the river, or the sea for that matter, in fact not even a duck pond lay on our route. This was becoming interesting I thought but James was more dubious. After some miles of travel, Jack indicated he was turning off the road, or country lane actually so I dutifully followed and found, yep! We were in a field.

I followed Jack with some trepidation now, hoping I would not get stuck in the mud, the weather had been wet of late and the ground was a tad soggy. At last Jack stopped his car at the far end of the field and climbed out with a wide grin. James and I did the same, though without the silly grin and in moments we were stood beside Jack wondering where the heck the boat was. With a flourish, Jack waving his arm in the general direction of a hedge before walking off towards the said vegetation. James and I followed, still unsure of what to expect and still no sign of the boat we had come to view. Jack finally came to a halt a few yards from the hedge right in front of a large bramble patch.

'Here we are,' announced Jack, 'I'll just clear it a bit then you'll get a better view.'

A better view I wondered? I had not even glimpsed a square inch of the boat yet, what did he mean by a better view. A better view of what? I watched as Jack pulled a pair of thick gloves from his back pocket and began tearing at the brambles. Within a few moments he had cleared enough away for me to make out a section of blue tarpaulin beneath the foliage. Several more clumps of brambles were ripped apart or pushed aside and a blue lump gradually came into view.

'You could help,' grunted Jack as he continued his labours.

'Help with what? What's under there?' I asked though suspicions were rising slowly in my mind.

'The damn boat is under this lot! Help me clear some of this stuff outta the way and you'll soon see. It's under the tarpaulin. I covered it when I stored it here.'

'How many decades ago was that?' I enquired.

'Funny! It hasn't been here long, maybe a year or so. I've just not had the time to use it. The farmer who owns this field is a friend and said I could keep it here for as long as I wanted. But like I said, I've not had the time and now the missus wants me to get rid of it. There we go, that's better, if we trample down the brambles now, we'll be able to get the tarpaulin off. It's a grand boat you'll see. It's a shame I have to get rid of it really.'

Yeah right, here we go I thought, out comes the sad story of how he will miss the boat and how reluctant he is to sell it. Anything to get the price up a bit I suspected. Fat chance I concluded. For the next few minutes or hours, I lost track of time, all three of us pulled, kicked and trampled our way through the brambles until a clear mound was evident. There in front of us sat a large blue mound, giving no clue whatsoever of what lay beneath. In a united effort to free the land locked vessel from the clutches of Mother Nature, we all grabbed a section of the tarpaulin and pulled. In a moment the vessel in all its glory was revealed and James and I stood back to encompass the view. A view that consisted of a pile of dead leaves mixed with twigs and other natural detritus littering the surface structure on top of a green hull. At that moment a red faced young couple suddenly appeared from the back of the boat next to the hedge. Obviously they had crept in between the mound of thorns and the field hedge in order to pursue those activities young members of opposing sex enjoy. I did not recognise either the boy or the girl, but possibly I will always remember the sight of those rosy red buttocks rapidly disappearing across the field as the couple fled with their clothes grasped in a bundle under their arms. Several moments passed as we all contemplated the vanishing pair before Jack dragged us back to the subject in hand.

'I'm afraid I haven't cleaned it for a while,' apologised Jack, 'but I promise you it's a lovely boat.'

I simply could not reply, afraid I may spoil our friendship with what I considered would be a suitable reply. James however had no such concerns and gave a loud snort of derision. With a sigh at our reaction, or lack of it on my behalf, Jack turned and rushed back to his car before reappearing several moments later armed with a hand brush, a container of water and several rags. Dumping the cleaning materials beside a totally flat tyre attached to the sad looking trailer upon which the boat sat, Jack grabbed up the brush and began sweeping all the debris off the surface of the boat.

'Come on you two, lend a hand. It won't take long to clean it up a bit then you'll see what a good boat it is,' urged Jack.

So with some reluctance James and I picked up a rag each and set about removing the compost covering the craft. When all the loose material had been cleared off, Jack poured water from the container into a small bucket and added some cheap looking cleaning fluid. We all soaked our rags in the liquid and attacked the green mould that cloaked the boat in an effective natural camouflage. After a period of sweating we had cleaned enough of the boat to gain our first real look at the thing. It was no longer a green compost heap in the corner of a field. Before us now sat a vessel about fourteen feet long with a white hull. Or a nearly white as it would need a lot more cleaning to return it to its original state. It had a small blue cuddy on the bow with a hatch at the front which allowed access to the bow and anchor fittings. A painted bow rail offered a minuscule sense of security for anyone brave enough to venture out onto the very small bow and that was about it.

I suppose I could say it resembled a Dejon 14 but only loosely, very loosely in fact. Whereas the Dejon has a square shaped cuddy, this boat possessed a rounded form of cuddy, only big enough inside for two people to shelter from the wind. There was a narrow wooden door attached but this had seen many better days and fell off as soon as James went to open it. The hull was smooth and curved as most hulls; it did not have the imitation clinker that the Dejon sported. Other than the fact that it did not actually resemble a Dejon, the overall size was there at least.

The boat was of GRP or glass reinforced plastic construction. In the cockpit, that area where one stands in the cold, rain, wind and waves while steering. Storage units that also served as seating ran along each side of the inner freeboard and continued into the cuddy before joining at the bow section. There was no seat or other fitting at the stern, the uncluttered transom remaining free for the use of an outboard motor. In truth the boat proudly displayed by Jack was basically an open fishing boat with a small cuddy perched on the bow. Ideal for what I thought at that time was what I wanted. Jack had already informed me that he had a five horse power Mercury outboard engine to accompany the boat. This I could live with as by now I was quite familiar with the Mercury engine; however I had yet to see the thing. If the condition of the boat was anything to go by, I expected the engine to be a rusting and corroded hulk of plastic and metal.

But my concentration was on the little boat and to be honest, following a superficial cleaning, the thing did not look too bad. Even James was coming round to the fact that this was a different sort of boat, no gleaming varnish with stainless steel fittings or soft bunks, or a toilet, or a cooker and was approximately six foot shorter than our last boat. But so far his experience had only been on the Lundy Mist, a sea sickness inducing catamaran or the fine sailing sloop of my friend Don. His overall impression did brighten when he realised that a boat such as this required less maintenance and much less work that a sailing yacht. Not that he did any work on the boats anyway, but the idea of less maintenance still cheered him. All there was to do on this type of boat was start the engine and wave a fishing line at any passing fish.

Once James and I had examined the boat closely, the arguing over its price began. Jack obviously wanted as much as possible whereas I wanted to pay as little as possible. Finally we reached an agreement in which I believed I came out the winner. But then everyone tends to assume they have won a hard fought battle when actually, they have paid exactly the figure both parties had in mind before the onset of the verbal posturing known as haggling. I did set a few conditions though, after James had whispered a reminder. We agreed that any exchange of money would depend on Jack making the trailer roadworthy again and the condition of the Mercury engine. Jack agreed and with the deal concluded, we left the field and retied to the local hostelry for refreshments.

A few days later found the vessel parked on its trailer outside our house. A sight that drew many comments about flooding and did I think I was Noah. I ignored them all with a haughty pose and set to work with a scrubbing brush, a rag and a bucket full of all purpose cleaner. As predicted, there was not a great deal of work needed, in fact it was mostly just cleaning. By the time my hands were red and wrinkled the boat sat gleaming in the autumn sunshine. The Mercury engine was safely stored in my shed and I had already taken a cursory look and decided it seemed fine. I had managed to get it started with the aid of a new set of spark plugs and fresh fuel. By placing the propeller and lower section of the shaft in a large bucket filled with water, I had managed to run the thing for a few moments and it sounded healthy. But my Seagull always sounded healthy, until one got it out on the water, then it would suddenly become sick. Damn thing!

As for the trailer, Jack had pumped up the tyres and removed any lingering brambles and Triffids but I still needed to check and grease its wheel bearings and tow hitch. All in all it was in reasonable condition and appeared capable of transporting the boat the two miles from my home down to the river. Once the boat was on the river, the trailer would be stored at home and only used on the odd occasion when the boat came out of the water. Over winter I hoped to store the boat itself in my other berth which was off the river with the water only reaching it during the high tides. It was the exact same place where I had kept and worked on the Lundy Mist. This left me plenty of time to fiddle and potter about with it without bringing the wrath of my wife down upon my head by keeping the craft outside my front door.

As I have mentioned, I wished for a low maintenance and low expense vessel and with this little boat I certainly got it. We decided to name the craft *Passion Flower* for no other reason than memories of the young couple we had disturbed when uncovering the boat. It had no name when we took possession; Jack it seems could not be bothered and simply called it, The Boat. Yeah I know, very original but I suppose such a name would be easy to remember. And in truth when sailors and other assorted boating people mention their craft to others, they do mostly call their craft, the boat. I for one always tend to announce that I am going down to the boat. I seldom if ever state that I am going to the Lundy Mist or the Yellow Peril. So with a bottle of beer and the help of a few neighbours, we named the vessel in a short but meaningful ceremony and from then on the little boat rescued from the clutches of brambles and hidden in a field was known as the Passion Flower.

Talking about low maintenance, the Passion Flower did have the odd drawbacks in my opinion. While it did possess a cuddy of sorts, it did not have the remote control unit, in other words any gear and throttle levers near the cuddy. In fact it did not have any form of controls at all. One simply sat or stood near the stern and controlled the boat via direct contact with the outboard engine. Now this is fine normally, most regular boaters like to stand in the boat as it gives a much better view of any nearby vessels, floundering submarines or rogue blue whales that may enter the river in search of an ice cream treat. I myself often prefer to stand with one hand clutching the control arm of the engine and initially I saw no issue with this arrangement. Until it rained of course, or when the wind increased in strength or the temperature dropped, then the ability to steer the boat from inside a cabin or at least behind the shelter of the cuddy was a definite advantage to ones wellbeing and enjoyment of the pastime. However this was a very small concern and I was thankful for the fact that the boat had one less thing to breakdown. Anyway, the Lundy Mist and even the Yellow Peril required the helmsman to brave the elements when manning the tiller, so I was quite used to freezing wet hands and face by then.

The other drawback was entirely down to Jack's fishing ambitions. On board the small fourteen foot Passion Flower day boat I discovered a fish finder that could not find a fish in a fish tank, a depth finder that thought the river was an ocean and a compass that appeared to be totally lost. Wires littered the cuddy and holes in the structure of the cuddy indicated where Jack had attempted to fit these models of modern technology. I quickly ascertained that Jack was no electrician and neither did he have any skills regarding the location and fitting of these instruments. I wondered why someone would place so much equipment on such an unsecured vessel and why would anyone need all these instruments on such a small boat. I removed the lot and sealed up the holes. Not to keep the weather out of course, the lack of a door made that unnecessary anyway. I filled the holes simply for ascetic purposes. I did not wish to own a boat that appeared to have woodworm! I did decide to replace the door but considered that was a chore that could wait for another day. As the whole vessel was GRP, a bit of rain would certainly not hurt it. Finally the Passion Flower was a ready as it could be. The trailer was roadworthy in a manner of speaking and the engine working, again in a matter of speaking. So one sunny but cold day, James and I hitched the trailer and boat to our car and headed off down to the river for our maiden voyage in our new boat.

Reversing the trailer down the small slipway, we launched the Passion Flower into the water, the first water other than rain it had seen in more than a year, according to Jack that is. I personally felt the boat had not floated for several years but it did not matter, it was ready, it was on the water and it was floating. James held the boat at the side of the slipway while I parked the car and trailer and then we set off for our first adventure aboard the little plastic boat grandly named Passion Flower. I had brought a pair of oars with me, in fact I seldom went anywhere on a small boat without the reassurance of oars. I now used the oars to push our boat away from the slipway and into water deep enough to use the engine. Surprisingly it actually started and we took off to explore the river, become familiar with our new boat and try hard not to sink it.

The day went well, much to my own surprise and James's expectant enthusiasm. The motor purred happily and pushed us on our journey with no coughs, splutters or breakdowns. The boat itself remained afloat and although the weather was a tad chilly, the sun shone down on us. Obviously the Gods of the water were content to allow us to continue, probably saving all the mishaps and malfunctions for another day. The Passion Flower was easy to handle and responded well to the direction of the engine and to the swell of the river. I felt safe enough but as usual, James could not care a jot, he was having fun. James took his turn at controlling the boat, a fact I was delighted with as I feared the episode with the catamaran had put him off taking the helm for ever. At last after two happy hours motoring here and there upon the water, we turned the bow towards the slipway and headed back to shore.

We had not taken any fishing equipment on that day as we wanted to test our boat fully, without the added distraction of attempting to catch the single elusive fish that may have strayed unwittingly into our section of the river. So all we had to occupy ourselves was putting the boat and its motor through as many paces as we could conceive. Happily it passed all our tests and we knew we had a nice little boat capable of withstanding our amateur attempts at marine recreation. Our hopes for the following years boating had received a boast at last.

Winter struck in earnest and the weather became slightly wetter and colder than summer so the boat was left on the drying mooring with occasional visits by myself to bail it out and remove the obligatory seagull presents. I enjoyed visiting the drying moorings because many of my boating friends also moored up in that location during the winter. Inevitably a group of us would end up gathered around someone's boat as we chatted about local issues and put the world in general to rights with our own individual opinions and suggestions, before taking the discussion off to the local pub and a liquid lunch. I relished my trips to check the boat, even when no one else appeared to distract me from whatever chore I had intended to do. The main job during this time was the dreaded anti-fouling. This is a heinous task that requires repeating every season. The anti-fouling keeps barnacles, crustaceans and limpet mines from attaching to the hull and slowing the boats speed and ease through the water.

Those days working alone in the tranquillity of the river side were a delight to me, apart from grovelling under the boat in the sticky black mud while being splattered with the obnoxious anti-fouling of course. The other chores I undertook that winter were minimal, mainly fitting the odd extra cleat or light fitting. I did splash a bit of paint around, just to brighten it up but it was the peace and solitude I really enjoyed. Wrapped up well in jumpers and coats with at least two pairs of socks squeezing my feet inside my Wellington boots against the cold, I marvelled at the wildlife and beautiful winter scenery around me. Woollen hats, scarves and thermal fingerless gloves enabled me to continue working on the boat or its mooring ropes through the gloom of winter while I waited for the promise of summer returning.

Chapter Eleven: Passion Flower.

Surprisingly summer did return to the cold and wet British Isles, or at least the temperature rose a few degrees and the rain no longer came down in shards of ice. I had finished all the chores on board the Passion Flower and had often become covered in mud from head to foot as I undertook the very last chore and applied the necessary anti-fouling paint to below the water line. This a is job every boatman or sailor hates, anti-fouling paint is an unpleasant substance and unless one has their boat propped up on legs or in a cradle, then some unfortunate individual has to climb under the boat and lay on their back while trying to avoid getting a mouthful or eye full of the evil stuff as it drips off the brush. As it was my boat, this chore obviously fell to me and I duly became plastered in mud, seaweed and a fetching shade of copper from the anti-fouling. The foul stuff lay in puddles on the ground for me to lie in and managed to get up sleeves, down trouser legs and in all sorts of hidden places that one would not believe possible.

I had purchased an anchor and a suitable length of rope on which to secure it to the boat. An anchor is always handy to have around, even if one is only sailing on a river, estuary or garden pond. A breakdown can occur anywhere and at any time, sinking the anchor allows one to make repairs or scream for help without the added threat of drifting into another vessel, into rocks or off the edge of the world. However as with any tool or piece of equipment, it is only as good as the person using it, and sometimes that person is an idiot. I had also fitted a set of navigation lights with any possible night trips in mind. I knew I would most likely never use them but they looked good and gave me the impression I knew what I was doing. A red light was attached to the port or left side of the boat as one is looking forward over the bow. I have always remembered a little ditty to help recognise which side is which when it comes to navigation lights. The ditty is as follows, "The Captain *LEFT* his bottle of *RED PORT* behind." Maybe not the best example but it has always worked for me and so certain my memory was correct, I then fixed the green light to the starboard or right side of the boat. Finally I secured a plain white light to the stern, making sure it was not obscured by the outboard motor. I purchased a small motorcycle battery to power the lights, being only a quarter the size of a car battery meant there was less chance I would trip over it and head butt the water on my way to the bottom.

Prepared for anything now, the time for launching approached. I say launching but as the Passion Flower was actually still at the river's side; it was more a case of a floating it off the mud and out to my berth on the river itself. All went well and I was proud of my new little boat. Fourteen foot is a good size for pottering about on the river and I could stray out of the harbour mouth onto the sea. Providing the weather was calm, the water flat and no wandering tsunami's prowled the coastline, waiting for the unsuspecting amateur boat person wallowing about on the water. I said a fourteen foot boat was a good size, however once on the open expanse of the river itself, both the Passion Flower and I began to feel very small and insignificant out amongst the big boats and deeper water. However I shrugged my shoulders, started the engine and scuttled off for an hour of mindless marine manoeuvres while further testing out the Passion Flower. I was learning all its quirks in the knowledge that if anything did go haywire, it would only be me that met Davy Jones and not any family or friends. However old Davy must have been in a good mood that day because I survived, in fact I not only survived but I actually had fun.

After my adventures on the Lundy Mist, Don's sleek sloop and the sickening catamaran, the ease and handling of the Passion Flower was a welcome contrast. Basically all I had to do was sit comfortably, or at least as comfortable as possible on hard and cold plastic seating, and steer the craft where ever I wished to go. As I motored along the river, it soon became apparent that although some of the more arrogant sailors in their massive gin palaces deemed me and my small vessel unworthy of acknowledging, my boating friends could not have cared less. It did not matter what form of craft I owned as long as I was out on the water. It was not long before I had been hailed to join a small group of boats tied together down river with the obligatory cans of lager in evidence. Steering towards the floating bar, I tied the Passion Flower alongside a twenty foot long motor cruiser named The Diving Otter. I am not sure what make of boat it was, suffice to say it was a motor cruiser with all the aspects of that form of craft. As I tied my tiny boat to the towering gunnels of The Diving Otter, I realised just how small my boat was. In fact I had to climb up almost three foot to get aboard the other craft, without any aid from the drinkers already aboard. There were three others sat around with cans in their hands and each one watched me clamber over the side rails with I suspected, a secret wish that I ended up in the water. No malice intended though, they simply yearned for some entertainment, albeit at my expense. I failed to amuse them I am happy to say.

I spent a very pleasant hour chatting with my fellow boating buddies before climbing down into the Passion Flower once more. I had received many positive comments regarding my new craft and left feeling less concerned about the size of my craft. I suppose it is a man thing, always wanting something bigger than the next man, but I concluded that quality was better than quantity. A weak excuse used mainly by men I admit, but the excuse comforted me at that time. With my boosted confidence I decided to continue down river to the harbour. If I could survive the huge size and the large numbers of other vessels scurrying about me, including kamikaze holiday sailors, impatient ferrymen and cargo vessels full to the gunnels with Chinese imports, I knew I would be satisfied with the Passion Flower. So I held my head high and ventured into the fray. I failed to consider the possibility of my bravado being a direct result of the one or three cans of the amber nectar I had consumed during the river gathering earlier. However I was soon reminded by the onset of a natural but very desperate need.

By the time I had reached the destination of the harbour, I resembled a contortionist. The three lagers had taken their toll on my body and now my bladder screamed at me for release. If I was still pottering about in the seclusion of the river I could have stood over the gunnels with the wind behind me, but here in the heavily populated harbour I had no avenue of escape. Boats of all shapes and sizes moved through the water about me, ahh water, that thought only made my need more desperate. Speeding up the engine I steered in agony towards the floating pontoon that allowed access to the shore. I thanked my lucky stars I now had a small and easily manoeuvrable vessel instead of the slower Lundy Mist. In moments that felt like years I found a vacant berth in amongst other craft less than fifteen foot in length and tied my bow mooring line to one of the stainless steel cleats on the pontoon. As soon as the knot was secure I shot from my boat in a blur, off at a knock kneed run towards to public toilets one hundred yards away. Running and scattering holiday makers and locals aside along the way in my mad dash to answer one of Nature's most urgent demands.

I am pleased to announce I arrived at my destination without any mishaps or accidents, in fact not even a dribble. My sigh of relief resounding from the old convenience brought many a smile of understanding from those passing by. At last my agonies were over and I realised I was hungry. Knowing my little boat was secure and would hopefully still be tied to the pontoon when I eventually returned, I gave way to a less demanding bodily urge and sought out a suitable refreshment venue. The fact that it also sold liquid refreshment was purely an aside, my main interest was food, honest! An hour passed in comfort and hospitality before I returned to the Passion Flower and was delighted to discover it still in situ and unharmed. Although boat theft is rare during daylight hours, it is not uncommon for a fellow boatman or sailor to 'borrow' a boat from the pontoon to make a short trip to and from their larger vessel moored on the river. Most locals understand this and many have even needed to partake of this strange custom themselves. One only has to wait and the craft will be shortly returned with gratitude from the temporary user. Fortunately for me, no one had chosen my craft and it sat patiently awaiting my return. Within minutes I was aboard, untied from the pontoon and with the engine started and chugging away happily, I turned the bow up river and headed towards my berth and home, satisfied with the Passion Flower and my day out.

My trip back up river was reasonably uneventful, apart from the result of the two drinks I had partaken of to wash down my meal at the restaurant, on top of and including the lagers consumed earlier of course. However once away from the prying eyes of the locals, the delighted eyes of bored holiday makers and the occasional hungry seagull in search of a small but tasty morsel wriggling about over the gunnels, I was able to relieve myself with impunity and privacy during the remainder of the trip. I must admit at this point that I was grateful not to have consumed a curry for lunch, especially that variety of curry famed for its connection to the consumption of lager. The demands of Nature may have had a more extreme effect on my body and created a demand that would not have been so easy to relieve! I had no loo roll on the boat and the bucket I kept on board was very, very small!

I was satisfied with the Passion Flower so a week or so later I managed to get my wife Joy and my son James to agree to a day out and picnic on the river. My daughter also decided to accompany us, a very infrequent occurrence indeed. So as a family we set off on the Passion Flower for a day out on the river. James and I had brought our fishing rods but in truth I did not expect to catch anything. I have fished on many occasions however I will be the first to admit that the fish are perfectly safe when I am about. Whether I have fished from the water side, from a quay or off a boat, my catches can be counted on one hand, one finger actually and that was only a garfish, not the most appealing catch of the day. James had more luck than I and was keen to learn the skills of an angler, and I was happy to encourage in this age old pastime. I considered it less dubious than some of the more modern pastimes pursued by young people these days.

On that day I decided not to amuse any passing fish with my feeble attempts to catch them, instead I concentrated on ensuring I steered to all the main features of the river, hoping to impress the female members of my family in a vain attempt to woo them into the delights of boating. I am not sure my plan entirely worked as it happened. I had checked over the Mercury outboard and other such important equipment such as a pair of oars, flask of tea and box of sandwiches and snacks, so I was reasonably satisfied that all would go well with our day out. With age and experience I now understand that when one is sure nothing can go wrong, that is when either Sod's Law or Murphy's Law or both will strike.

We motored up and down the river, making new sights our destination as we watched and marvelled at the wildlife and beautiful scenery that made up our immediate environment. Cormorants dived, fish leaped, Kingfishers fished and the surrounding woodland was alive with rustling sounds and the flutter of birds more suitable to land than water. No humans encroached into our little world as we pottered about the calm water of the river. All was right with the world, surely no one could grumble about such a day.

Leaving the wide section of quietly flowing water, we turned off and explored all the small creeks, inlets and channels of woodland and water that branched off from the main body of water, opening our eyes to new delights amidst the tranquillity of nature. We enjoyed our picnic on a tiny secluded beach seldom trod by human feet, sat on a grassy knoll and watch the water boatmen (the insect type) scurry about the water's surface while the silver shadows of fish prowled below, hoping to make a meal of the insects. We threw crumbs from our sandwiches onto the water and the surface rippled as small fish nibbled at the unexpected food. Sounds extremely idyllic, does it not? In truth it was and I was pleased to see that the other members of my family were smiling and happy as the day proceeded.

Heading back onto the busy main waterway, we motored down river for no other reason than the fact we could. The river soon became quite wide and the water surface rippled and rolled under the warm breeze and our hair ruffled with the forward motion of the boat as it travelled across the water. We had now been on the river for some time and I was enjoying myself, even the female family members appeared to be enjoying the day. My wife was busy photographing anything that ventured within camera range and I pointed out features of interest as we sailed along. James continued his efforts to catch us a fish supper while my daughter June had wisely brought a book and sat happily reading. It was a pleasant day in pleasant company amongst the natural wonders of the river. It all went pear shaped within seconds!

Suddenly the engine began to cough and splutter before dying a moment later. I realised the problem but felt no concern as I reached down for the petrol can. I knew the motor had run out of fuel so a quick refill and we would be on our way once more. I searched the can's normal position within the boat, my hands grasping thin air before realisation dawned. The petrol can was not there!

'Oh crap!' I exclaimed as the image of the can still sat on the doorstep at home flashed into my mind.

'What's up? What's wrong with the engine? Can you fix it?' called my wife's worried voice.

'Er not this time I'm afraid. We've run out of fuel. And I've forgotten to bring the fuel can,' I replied somewhat embarrassed.

Within moments of the engine stopping we had begun to drift. This would not normally be a problem because although this section of the river was constantly busy with passing craft, there were not usually any stationary vessels to crash into, except that day. A cry from James alerted me to the fact that we were drifting towards a gleaming white sloop that had anchored to one side of the river, probably to partake in refreshments as I could not see those on board as fishing types. With a flash of intelligence that surprised my anxious family and shocked the heck out of me, I stated that I would simply lower our anchor. This would enable us to remain stationary until a willing helper came our way. Without another thought I reached in one of the storage spaces, grasped the anchor and threw it over board. Now, remember I spoke about using an anchor earlier? Yes well it was a pity I did not listen to my own advice.

I knew the depth of water beneath our boat would be about fifteen feet so when I noticed the anchor line uncoiling at a rapid rate, I realised something was wrong.

'Did you tie on the other end of the line dad? James shouted as he lunged for the disappearing line, alas too late.

'Er no . . .' was my gutted reply.

We all watched in horror as the end of the anchor line vanished down into the depths. I had indeed forgotten to attach the end of the line to a cleat. Looking up I saw that the occupants of the sloop we were drifting towards had also witnessed my superior act of stupidity, and realisation played on their faces as a collision now appeared inevitable. James thought faster than I and immediately picked up one of the oars in readiness to shove us away from the other craft before we rammed into it. Seeing his action I grabbed the other oar and made ready to do the same. The trick is to gently nudge an oar against the hull of the stationary vessel and push away our boat before the two craft meet in full contact. We were within inches of our oars touching the other vessels hull when we suddenly stopped, causing me to almost fall. A fall that might have had disastrous consequences, I was perched precariously on the bow of the Passion Flower and leaning way too far over the bow rail in an attempt to lengthen the reach of my oar. Wondering why we had stopped, I looked up and saw a gentleman from the other vessel holding a long boathook which he had jammed against our bow, just below the gunnels. The gentleman was grinning and I wondered what the real reason for that grin was. It was most likely that he was relieved to have stopped us ramming his posh boat, however in my mind I could not help but notice his boathook was much longer than my oars. I think it is a man thing again but I suddenly felt somewhat inferior at the length of his equipment.

With expert ease the grinning gentleman guided our craft round to the side where willing hands placed fenders between us before securing the Passion Flower to its much bigger, more expensive and far better equipped companion. Once secured and polite introductions made, the grinning gentleman - oh how I wished he would stop grinning - enquired what the problem was. With a reddening face I was forced to admit I had forgotten to bring along any extra fuel for our engine. A crime only the most inapt sailor would commit, and the faces peering down at me from the sloop mirrored my own conclusion. I was that inapt sailor in their eyes.

'Oh that's easy to fix,' replied the grinning man, 'I always carry a can of petrol for my spare outboard. You are welcome to take what you need to get you home.'

'That's very kind of you,' I replied while ignoring his obvious reference to him being more prepared than I was. 'I am happy to pay for what I use if you wish?'

'No, no there's no need for that. I'm glad to help, hang on a moment and I'll get my can.'

With that he left the side from which he had grinned down at me and went to collect his fuel can. In a moment he returned and passed down his petrol can to me, while still grinning I might add. I quickly filled the engine tank halfway before passing the can back to him. Once my hands were free again I gave our engine a few pulls and it eventually coughed back into life. The other members of his crew or party swiftly untied the two vessels and once more we were on our way. We returned their waves and I called across that I would buy the drinks next time we met. He grinned even broader if that was physically possible and stated he would accept my invitation next time he was in our area. I speeded the engine up, eager to escape that grin as we motored back to our berth about a mile up river. Talk on our boat was minimal on the return trip. I think my wife was quietly fuming with embarrassment and I knew I was in for an ear bashing once we got home. My daughter was now huddled inside the cuddy, her looks told me that all the good work I had done to convince her that boating was fun had quickly evaporated during our little mishap. James however could not have cared less; it was just part of the whole adventure as far as he was concerned. As for myself, I prayed I would never see that grinning face again, nevertheless I was extremely grateful for his act of kindness, and his fuel of course.

Chapter Twelve: A return to sail.

Following our little episode with the anchor and running out of fuel, I tried to explain to my wife and daughter that we had not been in any danger when the motor stopped. I pointed out that I had remembered to take along the oars and if necessary I could have rowed our boat back to its mooring. However I did not admit that rowing the mile or so back up river would have totally knackered me, probably killed me in fact. I certainly would not have made the distance without serious concerns for life and limb. I thought it prudent not to mention that minor detail. June, my daughter remained unconvinced and it took some persuading and no little bribery to get her on the boat again. Funnily enough, I always remembered to take along extra fuel after that, sometimes it takes me a while to learn anything that may relate to common sense.

The Passion flower provided James and I with hours of fun for the next couple of years and even my wife Joy accompanied us on a few occasions - surprisingly. It was a nice little boat, easy to handle and moor up after a day on the water. We did manage to venture out onto the open sea when the weather was fine and the sea was calm. I did not consider it a big enough boat to tackle any swells larger than a foot or two, but it never let us down and we remained safe within its embrace. Many fishing trips were undertaken on board the Passion Flower, though I admit I seldom took part in this strange activity. I remember the old proverb that stated, `*Give a man a fish and he will eat for a day. Teach him how to fish and he will sit in a boat & drink beer all day.*'

I was happy to take friends out fishing and James enjoyed a battle with the denizens of the deep, but I remained inept at catching anything other than a cold. Mackerel were the main catch of the day, trailing a mackerel line across the small bay in which the harbour was situated appeared to be a favourite spot for these fish. It was so easy to catch mackerel that one almost did not need a fishing line, if one shouted I am sure they would leap into the boat all by themselves. I did not catch any.

The river on which we enjoyed the delights of the aquatic world was not high on fish stocks. Some fish such as Bass were situated here and there along with shellfish such as oysters, least I think they were oysters, they had shells anyway. I was informed that other species like flounder and even salmon inhabited the water but with my fishing skills I never managed to verify the claim. I did once entice something onto my fishing hook but alas when hauled into the boat, it turned out to be a clump of mussels, an edible bivalve mollusc so my dictionary informs me, clinging to a tangled web of seaweed. Normally I did not even catch a discarded Wellington boot or supermarket shopping trolley, but at least I managed to pull some mussels. Fishing trips and pleasure trips were the main purpose of the Passion Flower, along with the odd excursion down river to the harbour and the small town that surrounded it. My wife accompanied me quite frequently, it appears she trusted small boats and disliked the larger ones. Her reasoning was that she felt safer in a small boat, strange I know but that was her conclusion. I would much rather be on an ocean going liner than a fourteen foot craft, however I have always aimed my ambitions way too high. James still very much enjoyed the boating life and did partake in a spot of fishing when the situation arose, and it was on one such occasion when a fish caught me.

My neighbour and his son were very keen anglers so one fine day, James invited the neighbours boy called Andrew, to accompany us out on the river so Andrew could get his first experience of river fishing. James and Andrew were of a similar age and as they were close neighbours, they had become friends. Andrew's parents were happy for him to accompany us and Joy said she would come too. So with all the appropriate equipment, the four of us headed out for the day. Joy had packed enough food for an army as usual which included a large flask of coffee and a pack of fizzy drinks; just to keep the energy levels of two boys up you understand. James and I had our own fishing rods while Andrew borrowed his father's. It was not really suitable for boat fishing, being a long thin whippy thing but it would do. James and I both owned the shorter and more study style of rod, more suitable for use on a boat. My wife Joy simply took along a book, I think I should have done the same.

James and I had taken Andrew and his dad out fishing once before in a previous year, a trip riddled with disasters on Andrew's behalf if I remember correctly. The young lad had managed to hook himself several times, me once and the outboard motor frequently. He also had the dubious knack of tangling his fishing line with almost every cast he made. His poor father had little opportunity to do any fishing himself as Andrew required constant attention. Knowing this I was still happy to take him along, although he would certainly not get the kind of attention from me that he demanded from his father. Plus I hoped that the peer pressure of having James alongside may encourage Andrew to fend for himself and not wave his hook and line around like a demented windmill. I did not mind attaching the Lugworm or Sandeel to his hook but after that he was on his own. Luckily James held no such qualms and loaded his own line without following my example of stabbing my fingers with the hook.

Off we set, heading down river to a wide section that many other anglers used, a point I had noted on my trips up and down the river. I of course had no idea what type of fish they were attempting to catch but as many appeared to favour that spot, I thought I would give it a try. My fishing knowledge was so miniscule I would not have noticed fish in a tank, never mind in a wide river. With my second new anchor gripping firmly to the river bed and attached

215

securely to the boat this time, we set about readying the fishing equipment. I first ensured James and Andrew were fully equipped and had their lines over the side of the boat before casting out my own. Almost immediately I had to draw my line back in and free Andrew's line from mine, he had managed to allow his line to drift over mine somehow. It was a gift I suppose, being able to find and tangle two lines that were initially some distance apart. Casting out again, I let my line stretch out in the flow of the water and settled down for a long, boring and fruitless fishing experience.

Joy had made herself comfortable in the cuddy and was engrossed in her book so I gazed dreamily at the surrounding beautiful scenery and allowed my mind to wander. James and Andrew talked incessantly about all things young boys talk about, interrupted occasionally by James having to sort out Andrew's line, bait or whatever Andrew laid his hands on. I was very glad I had James along; if left to me I would probably have thrown Andrew over board long ago. The morning passed peacefully with nary a fish in sight, not unexpected for me but both boys normally caught something, but not today it seemed. Suddenly a loud rumbling echoed throughout the boat and both Joy and I looked up knowingly.

'Is anyone hungry by any chance?' enquired Joy.

'Me!' cried Andrew.

'Me too,' responded James already placing his rod in one of the rod holders.

Jack had claimed to be a very keen angler and certainly owned more fishing rods than anyone I knew. During his ownership of the Passion Flower he had attached four eighteen inch long tubes, cut down aluminium pipes I think, to each side of the stern for the purpose of holding fishing rods and it was these holders in which we all inserted our rods now. Within seconds the two boys were sat side by side in the cuddy opposite my wife, and more importantly, very near the food that was now being unwrapped. Soon the sound of munching floated over the water. I had also placed my rod in one of the holders but had failed to reel in my line, no point I thought as I reached for a sandwich, I had been holding it for over an hour and not threatened anything in that time. I forget what was in the sandwich but I enjoyed it I think, but it was the hot coffee that really hit the spot, I had not realised how thirsty I had become, surrounded as I was by all that water.

I was sipping coffee and munching a sandwich so I did not notice the strange noise at first. In fact it was not until Joy began staring towards the back of the boat that I retrieved my snout from the trough and turned to discover what had caught her attention. Both boys were still chatting while attempting to demolish every single morsel of food within arms reach. They were oblivious to the world about them, as usual with children it seems these days. Still with no comprehension of what my wife was watching, I glanced around the river for signs of disturbance or anything out of the ordinary. I failed to see any pirate ships, streaking mermaids or hands clutching a sword rising from the water so I still had no idea what could possibly be of such interest. All these responses and glances took but a second or two to register and less than a minute passed before I turned back to my wife and asked her what she was staring at.

'Can't you see it?' she said.

'See what?' was my typical husband's reply.

'Look at your rod, stupid!'

'Oh!'

She was right; my rod was jumping and wiggling about in its holder as if it had a life of its own. The line was still in the water where I had left it, but now it appeared to be attempting to escape the proximity of the boat. At that moment the two boys took notice and James jumped from his seat with a wide grin.

'I think you've caught a fish dad!' he exclaimed.

In some confusion I muttered, 'Me? No, I just put my rod in there while I had my lunch. I've not done anything to catch a fish. But it's certainly very mobile and we are not moving so something's caught in it, maybe some seaweed again. Let's have a look anyway.'

James reached my rod before me and leaned over the stern of the boat, peering down into the water. 'I can't see anything dad. Reel your line in slowly so we can get a better look.'

Reaching over him, I eased the rod from its holder and gently began turning the reel to bring the line in. In truth I expected to find a piece of branch or other debris caught up in the hook and being moved about by the tide. Slowly I reeled the mysterious object in, I may have hoped for a treasure chest but felt some doubt as to my luck. Inch by inch the line came up until James shouted that he could see something on the hook but did not know what it was. Suddenly the line and its captured cargo burst from the water's surface. It was a fish! A ten inch mackerel was squirming and leaping upon the fishing hook as I lifted it from the water. No one aboard was more surprised than me at the sight of an actual fish on my hook.

'Quick dad, put it in here,' shouted James as he grasped my bailing bucket, dipped it over the side into the water and placed the full bucket on the cockpit deck. With some presence of mind, Joy threw me an old rag in order that I could hold the fish without it slipping from my fingers. Carefully I eased the hook from its mouth and let the fish slide into a water filled bucket. There it sat, or lay or did what ever a fish does in the bucket, while the four of us stared down at it.

'What do we do with it?' asked Andrew with a gleam in his eye, 'Maybe we should kill it and eat it?'

'Why? It's only one little fish, it's not big enough for a decent meal,' answered James.

'Oh just throw it back in the water, the poor thing,' muttered Joy as she watched the fish attempt to swim in the small bucket.

'Nah, let's kill it!' continued Andrew.

James had been watching the fish also and concluded, 'No, mum's right, let it go dad.'

'Yeah I think so,' I agreed, 'no use in having just one fish. However, someone take a photo of it first. I'm gonna frame it, it's the only damn mackerel I've ever caught and I want proof.'

'But you didn't catch it dad, it caught itself!' grinned James.

'Shush, no one will know. Just take the picture.'

So Joy pulled out her small camera and snapped a picture for posterity of the little fish in the bottom of the bailing bucket.

'There!' she said, 'Now you have proof that you're not such a completely incompetent angler. Though I doubt anyone who knows you will believe it. Now put the poor thing back into the water before Andrew eats it raw!'

Following the instructions of my wife, just like all dutiful husbands do, I leaned over the gunnels and gently sank the bucket into the water and allowed the very relieved fish to swim away. This little episode had stirred the interest and vain hopes of the boys and they immediately returned to their own rods and cast out the lines. I said nothing; I did not want to disillusion them with the truth. Any fish that was stupid enough to get itself caught so far up river, was probably also quite lost. It was very unusual for a mackerel to come so far up river and away from the sea. If it had swum any further up river it would have found itself moving into fresh water. I am not an expert but I do not think mackerel are designed for fresh water. Secretly I considered the small mackerel to be the equivalent of a human plonker. I could not foresee any other, more intelligent fish swimming away from its home in the sea and then happily biting a dangling and stationary fishing hook. We did not catch anything else that day but it did not really matter to the two boys, one very little adventure was enough for them to regale their friends with when they returned to school. At the end of the day, the boys were happy, my wife was relieved we had made it back safe, and I was astounded we had survived the whole day without disaster, mayhem or accidents.

Although I enjoyed my time with the Passion Flower, I still felt I needed more. Simply motoring to and fro on the river with the occasional trip out of the harbour soon became routine, boring even. I had continued to sail with Don and eventually arrived at the conclusion that I missed sailing. Owning a small motor boat is very similar to driving a car. One went from A to B by starting and steering the engine, there was no real challenge. The trips out with Don were much more stimulating, especially when we were racing. Just a simple trip around the bay in Don's large Contessa involved some brain power and physical dexterity, enough activity to hold off any boredom.

James and I accompanied Don and his regular crew member Kevin out for a pleasure sail on a sunny Sunday in early summer one year. No route was planned as we decided to let whims take us to wherever as we headed out of the harbour and raised the sails. After some discussion it was agreed that we would sail to the opposite side of the bay, a trip of an hour or so depending on the strength of the wind. James of course was eager to use Don's mackerel line as he knew we would be sailing over the prime fishing grounds for these stripped fish. As for myself, I was content to assist with sailing the beautiful vessel, under instruction from Don or Kevin of course. As we were not racing or in a hurry to get anywhere, Don even allowed me to take charge of the tiller or rudder, what ever one wished to call it. I did not argue but I always thought the rudder was the bit in the water and the tiller was the arm one used to control the rudder. Whatever it was, I was put in charge of it. It is not as easy as some would think, steering a sailing vessel, one has to consider the wind direction, the tide and keeping the sails full of wind. However, under the guidance of Don and Kevin, I managed to avoid any serious mishaps and thoroughly enjoyed myself.

We sailed for a couple of hours before Don decided we should head back to the harbour. He had been keeping watch on the weather conditions and although the day remained bright and sunny, Don had noticed a sea mist was rolling in across the fetch. Being coastal dwellers, we all knew about sea mists. On the warmest of days a sea mist can quickly descend and cause the temperature to drop significantly, covering the coastline and blanketing the shore inland for several miles in a thick fog like cloud. One can be blinded by this form of mist a mile inland from the seashore, but if one travels but a mile further inland one will find a clear blue sky once more. Unfortunately if one is out on the water when a sea mist rolls in, it can become a serious concern as visibility drops down for just a few yards in moments. Not really ideal when one cannot see any other vessels heading in the same direction.

I once knew a guy who had bought a thirty two foot sloop, and enjoyed sailing it solo, even though he had no previous sailing experience. I think he bought the boat for prestige amongst his friends, rather than any real compulsion to take part in nautical activities. I enquired if his navigation skills were up to the task and was horrified by his reply. In complete earnest my friend replied that he was not concerned about mist or fog, even though he could not navigate or understand his array of instruments aboard the boat. He was reluctant to study a course in navigation because he stated, maths were difficult for him. I informed him that the maths involved were not that difficult but more importantly, his very life could depend on being able to read a chart and take bearings on his position. He shrugged off this small detail, saying that he would be fine. When I asked what he would do if caught in mist or fog, he stupidly tried to assure me that he would just know which way to steer, he would know which way to go. Obviously he had never been caught in such conditions at sea; there are no street lights, no direction signs or roads to follow. When out at sea in a fog or mist, one can see absolutely nothing, there is no indication at all of where the boat is, where the nearest port or harbour is, one can scarcely tell sea from sky. I vowed never to sail with him.

Having no navigation skills is not as uncommon as one would think. I once went out with my friend Steve. He owned a twenty something foot motor cruiser filled to the brim with fish finders, compasses, depth finders, logs and GPS (Global Positioning System). I had thought I would be quite safe as he gave the impression of being an experienced sailor or boat man, I was wrong. Leaving the harbour behind, I suggested we take the boat further out but Steve appeared very reluctant. When I pushed him for an explanation, he admitted he never went too far out to sea in case he could not find his way back. I was shocked at this reply because I had always thought that Steve was an old hand with boats. It turned out he had no navigation skills and nor did he understand all the array of instruments he had on board. I informed him that I could get him back and this brought an immediate smile to his face. Within seconds he had gunned the engine and we were heading for France!

'Ere, what happens if we run into some fog or mist?' he asked with a trace of concern in his voice that caused the obligatory hand rolled cigarette to tremble slightly in his thin lips.

I looked over at the tall and very thin figure of Steve, 'Shouldn't be a problem, you've got charts, a compass and a GPS so we'll just figure out where we are and make our heading from there. Honest Steve, there's no need to worry. Er . . we're not going deep sea, are we?'

I asked this because Steve was still powering his vessel rapidly out to sea and I had no idea where he was heading. Although I had no instruments on board the Passion Flower, I had passed the RYA navigation course and I had also learned a huge amount from Don. I was reasonably confident but I secretly prayed I would not be put to the test!

'France? Nah, not goin' there. They don't talk proper English!'

'Of course they don't, they're French that's why,' I retorted with a laugh.

'Well I don't bleddy care, if they can't speak like what we do, then I ain't going there. 'Er, where is France away?'

'Straight ahead if we continue on this heading,' I muttered, 'maybe slow down a bit and we'll figure out where you want to go.'

Thankfully Steve eased back the throttle and we slowed. Searching through his pile of Admiralty charts I soon found the one relevant to our area and laid it out on a bunk for examination.

I called Steve down into the cabin and pointed at a position on his chart. 'Okay Steve, this is where we are.'

Steve peered down at the chart then looked up and peered through one of the small cabin windows.

'I can see that, tis bleddy daylight and the day is clear 'nough for me to see them there cliffs and stuff. I know where we are, don't need piece o' paper to tell me where the heck I'm too.'

'Yeah I know Steve, good for you. But what I meant was we can also see where we are on this chart and with the GPS, it doesn't matter where we go; we can find our way back easily.'

'Huh! If you says so I suppose. So where we goin' then?' conceded Steve with a grunt.

Finally we agreed to head over to the next harbour about forty five minutes away across the bay. I think Steve was running out of tobacco and intended mooring up and nipping into one of the shops for more. Hell of a way to go for baccy I thought, but it was his boat after all. We did not need his charts or instruments that day as the weather remained clear and dry. However I did encourage Steve to get some lessons on navigation as soon as he could. Strangely he actually did, not by joining a class but by getting some of his fishing friends to teach him. I believe he is quite capable now and regularly ventures far out onto the sea, for fishing of course, or I suppose he could be off to buy cigarettes.

Our trip out with Don and Kevin had been extremely enjoyable, but now Don was growing concerned about the weather conditions. I fully trusted Don as he was a very experienced sailor and his boat was in top condition and fully equipped with all the instruments we would need to get safely home. However the wise sailor never takes anything for granted and so we turned about and headed back to the harbour some miles away. Suddenly the mist hit us and we were in a white out, not able to see more than a few yards around the boat.

Immediately Don swung into action, grasping the helm and shouting, 'Okay you lot, I want one of you on the bow and one each on either side of the boat. I am going to cut near to land so we can get out of this weather as soon as possible. Nevertheless there are some rocks under the surface and although I will cut round the headland, I can't be sure how close we'll be. So everyone keep an eye out for rocks and if you see one, shout out and I'll steer further away.'

So Kevin headed up to the bow as he was more experienced than James or me and lying down on the bow deck, he stuck his head over the side and stared down at the water. James and I followed suit and leaned over the side gunnels and freeboard in order to see the water beneath us. I admit I was tempted to dive into the heads (nautical term for toilet) as fear began gnawing at my stomach. I tried to reassure James but in vain, that daft sod was not scared at all, it was just another adventure as far as he was concerned. To be honest, James could swim like a fish and could easily make the shore if we struck a rock and began to sink. The sea was still very calm; it was only the lack of visibility causing our apprehension. I could swim all right; however swimming like a brick is not an ideal way of staying healthy so I was a tad nervous to say the least. Leaning far out over the side with the gunnels sticking hard into my gut, I prayed I would not see the black shape of a jagged rock beneath us as Don eased the boat forward. He had loosened the sails and now we were under engine power. Attempting fast turns and manoeuvres under sail is difficult and can take time, too much time to rapidly avoid tearing the bottom out of the boat. Staring down at the waters surface I began to feels quite nauseous, though to be fair, I was not sure if it was seasickness brought on by my close proximity to the water, or the fact that I was convinced I was going to meet Neptune at any moment.

A call from Kevin made Dom turn the boat out to sea a few yards more but other than that, we suffered no sinking or screaming or drowning and under Don's skilled boatmanship, we rounded the headland and moved into safer and deeper water. At last we could lift our heads from over the side as the threat of rocks had diminished. Visibility was still down near zero and Don was relying on his instruments and experience to get us back to the harbour. Another hour passed before the vague outline of the harbour appeared in front of us. As that wonderful sight, my stomach won and I rushed to the small and very compact heads, only to find a queue! It was evident that the others were not as brave or unconcerned as I had thought. Strangely Don got there first, shouting at Kevin to take the helm as he clambered down the few steps into the cabin. Unfortunately the one thing Don did not have on his well equipped vessel was – a can of air freshener!

As is always the case, the moment we entered the harbour, the mist cleared and we found ourselves once more under a clear blue sky, so bright it almost blinded us. Don raised the sails again and we pottered about the harbour for a while before finally heading back up river to Don's berth. All in all it was a good day, the minor scare created by the mist was soon forgotten and we were all in good spirits. Yet our small adventure had galvanised my old grey matter into action and I realised I missed the pleasure of sailing. I decided I would discuss the matter with the family when I got home. I wanted a sailing yacht again. I wanted the peace and quiet of wind power and the adventures that accompany the activity. A motorboat is fine but there is no challenge. One starts the engine, points the boat at where one wants to go and that is it really. A voyage under sail is totally different.

The hunt for another new boat began in the autumn; no one other than the most hardened souls or fishermen is particularly interested in water activities during the cold and wet months. What am I saying? This is Britain; summer is often only distinguishable from winter by the length of the day. Light but rain soaked evenings and weekends replace dark and rain soaked evenings and weekends. Disregarding the weather conditions, the winter months are the best time to purchase a boat as many people are totally fed up with them by then. A miserable summer ensures cheap vessels on the market almost as soon as the season ends. Spring is the worse time to purchase a boat. The promise of clear skies, dry weather and warm sunshine tempts the unwary innocent into dreams of sunny days on the water. Those innocents who assume owning a boat is a wish fulfilled or a gateway to a better life or a chance to get away from it all. The only thing that really gets away when owning a boat is money, your money, poured into that marine money pit. The cost of buying a boat will sink (*pardon pun*) as autumn wanes and winter takes a firm grip on all things important to a brass monkey. However the price begins to increase again along with the air temperature so one must strive to complete any deals before the first goose returns.

Following a few weeks advertising, I managed to sell the Passion Flower to yep, you have guessed it, to a keen angler and so I now had the funds to seek out a small yacht and plenty of time in which to do it. James and I looked at several boats over the next few weeks before settling on a seventeen foot sloop. With hindsight I may not have bought that vessel but I was too eager and my judgement had become clouded. The new boat, new to me that is, was a Pedro. Built by Florence Marine in the United Kingdom, the boat was a single mast vessel with seven foot beam. The hull was GRP and moulded in the clinker fashion. It had a small cabin which housed two berths, the promotion advert stated two to three berths but the third would only fit a very small child or the ship's dog. Unfortunately the Mercury was sold with the Passion Flower so unless I risked my old Seagull, I had no outboard as yet. The cabin had space for a galley but in truth, it was barely large enough so it remained empty apart from the berths. The Pedro was one of twins, its sister vessel was the Senorita with the main difference, or in fact the only difference being the keel that I could tell. The Pedro had one short stubby ballasted keel with two small bilge keels either side that allowed the boat to remain almost upright when out of the water. On the water it had an eighteen inch draft, ideal for river use. The Senorita had but one ballasted keel which was longer but as a result, the Senorita leaned over onto its side when on dry land. Otherwise the two vessels were almost identical, from above the water line they certainly looked the same. In the more equipped version of the Pedro a chemical toilet was available, however I found a bucket took up much less space. Finally the Pedro had the two main sails, a mainsail and a jib, with the option of a genoa for more speed. My new boat came with a full set of sails and the rigging and aluminium mast were in good order.

When I took possession of the Pedro it had a light blue hull and the obligatory white superstructure. Inside the cabin two blue coloured cushions rested on the main berths with a triangular cushion at the bow. Three windows allowed a good visage of the outside, one foreword and one each on either side. There was storage space beneath the berths. In the cockpit, similar seating ran three quarters of the cockpit length, leaving a space at the stern to swing the tiller which was attached to a wooden rudder. All in all the boat appeared to suit my needs, it was small and compact and more importantly, it was a simple design that would not test my sailing skills too much. The vessel did not come with a trailer but that was of no concern to me, I intended keeping it on my drying mooring beside the river. Luckily I had discovered the Pedro in the little hamlet from which I sailed, so all I had to do was float it around to my mooring, after handing over cash to the seller of course.

Over the winter months I worked on the Pedro, mostly cleaning but I did hoist the sails on one calm day. I had little experience in setting sails as Don obviously erected his own and on the Lundy Mist, I usually had assistance from John or any other willing crew member. I did of course help so I was not a total novice and the sails did eventually get up. I had been sailing and boating now for quite a few years and probably knew more than I gave myself credit for, but the responsibility of doing things right still worried me, a lack of confidence in my own abilities I realised. The rigging presented more of a problem, when I took ownership of the Pedro; the mast had been lowered in readiness for the winter, so I had to figure out the shrouds and halyards myself. In the main I managed quite well, I only slipped off the side and into the now very familiar mud once or twice, and I did not seriously hurt the passerby when I dropped the mast. It did not take me too long to comprehend that I could not hold up the mast and attach the rigging at the same time. Not unless I could quickly grow very long arms. So I enlisted the help of the stunned passerby and while he held the mast, I secured the rigging that held the mast upright. Eventually I considered the vessel seaworthy but what name was I to give it I wondered. It had a name, which escapes me now, but it was such a common name it was embarrassing. It is funny how every body appears to be under the elision that they were the first to come up with a name for their vessel, only to discover many others had had the same idea.

I originally considered a real manlike name, something like Destroyer or Terminator but let's be realistic, it was a small sailing boat, not a million pound super motor cruiser. Some after some consideration and taking into account the colour of the vessel; I decided to rename the boat, *Grumpy*. I think that was how I felt that day but I was slightly shocked when all my family commented on its appropriateness. So as spring approached, the Grumpy was ready and waiting to go. All we needed was some good weather. Several weeks later that weather arrived, for a day at least, and I took the Grumpy out of my winter mooring in readiness for the sailing season.

Chapter Thirteen: Sideways.

The Grumpy was clean, tidy and ready for its first experience of having me at the tiller, however other than the Seagull; I still did not have a suitable outboard engine for the craft. Remembering how reliable and efficient the Seagull was, I decided not to risk it. I did not want to get myself in bother by screaming obscenities at a useless inanimate lump of metal in the middle of the river. I did not have much cash available to invest in something new at that time and I would not consider hire purchase. I do not get into debt for anything that is not important to life and limb, such as a loaf of bread. Have you seen the prices of bread lately? So instead I trade, deal or beg those certain things in life that a man requires to maintain his soul. Important things like a boat, perhaps a motorcycle or an electric guitar that he will never learn to play. Luckily and after much searching and haggling, I managed to pick up what I was led to believe was a four horse power Sea Bee outboard quite cheap. I was unsure if it was actually a Sea Bee but it had a Briggs and Stratton engine which I understood. It was cream coloured and had a useful handle which ran around the entire engine; thus enabling me to turn the engine one hundred and eighty degrees to obtain reverse. If one did not rip out the stern with the propeller of course.

The little engine was light and easy to use, it remained in neutral gear while idling for starting but nothing else, so there was little to go wrong I thought. As it turned out, this small and identity unconfirmed engine proved it self reliable and would push the Grumpy easily through the water. Not certain I would not like to rely on it in heavy seas or perhaps even a strong breeze. But in truth would I be out on heavy seas? More than likely not, my seventeen foot sloop with its stubby keel was definitely more suited to calmer waters, it would never earn a place in the Fastnet race for sure. Arming myself with an oar just in case, a full set of sails and the Sea Bee engine, I set out on my maiden voyage in early April on the first fine day we had enjoyed for some time.

I kept to the river as I was alone for the initial trip and I did not yet have the confidence to risk battling the open sea. My choice of April was a wise decision as it was too early in the season for the hordes of holiday makers to descend on our river and coastline, but near enough to spring to allow some reasonable weather. By reasonable weather I mean of course drizzle instead of monsoons and a breeze rather than a gale. We Brits are a hardy bunch and the only thing that surprises us with the weather is when the sun comes out! On that day all I had to contend with were local boat enthusiasts cluttering up the river as they too tested out new vessels, or made their first trip out on boats repaired and cleaned over the winter months. Eager to join the early season throng, I slipped my mooring buoy. I used the alleged Sea Bee to move out into clearer water, away from the main mooring spots before switching it off and attacking the sails. Putting up sails and attaching rigging on ones own while bobbing about in a little boat on the water is no easy task. I managed to retain my footing and so avoided a soaking but the chore still took longer than I had hoped. Luckily none of my boating friends appeared to laugh hysterically at my efforts and I was left alone to make my mistakes.

Actually it was not too difficult to raise the sails, there were only two after all, and the main rigging including shrouds, forestays and spreaders had all been fitted when I put up the mast. But as is often the case, a simple task becomes a difficult chore in my hands. Neither sail was very large, the sail area was a lot smaller than the set I had on the Lundy Mist. Manhandling sails in a small boat on ones own is still a job to be reckoned with, but I bravely fought on until at last the main sail and jib were up, secured and ready to go. I learned a valuable lesson that day, set the sails up and leave them slack *before* slipping the mooring. Stupidity came easy to me, and still does I am told. Mainly by the wife of course but others appeared to share her opinion. Now the only question remained, was I ready? The Grumpy had drifted up river with the incoming tide while I tangled myself in sails and sheets so I eventually found myself in a wide section of water and floating towards a fork in the river. I was at a three way junction. I gave this fact absolutely no consideration as I tightened the jib sheet and the main sheet and embarked on sailing aboard the Grumpy.

I should have remembered my escapade aboard the Lundy Mist when attempting to sail in an area where the wind could swirl and gust from any direction. It was a short time later that I realised with a shock, I was actually sailing sideways! The little stubby keel under the Grumpy was not deep enough to bite properly into the water; it was only the weight of its lead filled construction that helped keep the boat upright. Asking it to help one stay on course was obviously a task to far. However I was now slightly more experienced so panic did not raise its head - much. I had sailed close the shoreline of the right hand fork, aiming to allow room for a straight sail across several hundred yards on the widest part of the river. I needed the practice before I ventured out to sea or even down river to the harbour for that matter. The Grumpy was quite easy to handle but not so easy to sail in swirling winds. When the question of how to stop it sailing sideways arose, it was a dilemma I had no immediate answers for. The water about me was empty so what ever I decided to do was down to me alone. The panic edged closer to the surface.

The shoreline consisted of mud banks in the main so I was not concerned for the safety of either the Grumpy or myself. My only real worry was becoming stuck and having to wait until a passing vessel could pull me out, and the embarrassment that would certainly follow. I tried wiggling the rudder as I had witnessed other sailors doing but to no avail, as yet I was not grounded but it would not be long. I tightened the sails in the hope that the wind would power me away from the shore, but again with no result. I scratched my head and pondered what action I could take to move my boat the few yards needed to get me away from the shore and back into a better wind. I considered chucking out my anchor and just sitting there, the section of the river in which I was stranded was quite busy, not as busy as it would be during the summer months, but at least some boats would be passing by during the course of the day I hoped. About two miles or so up river from my position near the right hand fork was situated a small hamlet and people often used to river to get to the harbour and its small town as the journey was long and arduous by road. I might well risk suffering a red face by seeking a tow after all.

Then I had an idea. I grasped the one solitary oar and attempted to push the boat out of the swirling wind and eventually catch some wind that was actually going in the direction I wanted. Another failure, the oar simply stirred up the muddy river bottom and annoyed a few fish. Surely someone would come along soon; all I needed was a small vessel as long as it had an engine . . . . . . An engine, oh damnit I had totally forgotten the engine!

Thankfully unlike the Seagull, the little Sea Bee kicked into life at the first pull and within moments I was heading away from the shore. Once a suitable distance away, I switched it off once more and resumed my sailing. I was feeling quite confident now I had remembered that the thing attached to the stern was in fact a reliable outboard motor and not a stray seal cadging a lift. I tightened the sails and tacked to and fro across the river, trying to make each tack or gybe faster and more efficient than the last. Gradually I learned the wind and how best to set the small sails in order to get the most speed from the vessel. I did not need the engine again as I stayed well away from the shore on each pass. I counted myself very lucky because even after a couple of hours on the water, no one had come along. It was obviously not a day for shopping or whatever it was people from the tiny hamlet sought down river. Eventually I grew bored of simply crossing the river endlessly so I turned the bow fully into the right hand fork with the intention of sailing up as far as I could before the water became too shallow. Alas it was not to be, I had travelled but a few yards into the smaller waterway when the wind dropped, my sails went limp and once again I was stationary. With a sigh

I restarted the engine and headed back out into the wider river. It appeared my newly gained experience did not out weigh my life time of stupidity. It was difficult enough sailing on the main river, attempting to sail on an even smaller waterway was out of the question. When I had motored back into the wind, I turned off the engine and sailed slowly back to my moorings. I was tired but delighted that I had enjoyed the day. I was also very thankful that I had not crashed, sunk or drowned during my initial excursion on the Grumpy.

Over that summer I sailed in the Grumpy as often as I could, it was quite an easy boat to handle so my confidence grew, though it still decided to go in every which direction quite often. I remained within the river and the harbour for much of the time out of pure cowardice, but I did venture out into the cold wet blue when ever I had the company of a more experienced sailor to guide me. In truth my skills were increasing and I could handle the boat on my own, however the sea is something not to take for granted so I felt happier when there was another aboard to balance out any stupid mistakes I might make. I have always been of the type who acts first and thinks later, so having someone onboard to watch over me was always an advantage to life and limb.

With all precautions taken, mostly by others rather than me, the season passed without any serious blunders or mishaps. I managed not to fall overboard, a miracle in itself, and other than cuts and bruises I did not require the rescue services. Eventually winter loomed closer and I reluctantly decided it was time to head for my safe mooring on the muddy banks of the river. I have described the mooring as being beside the river which no doubt has lead to images of a boat tied sadly to an overgrown grass bank that dropped down to the gently lapping waters edge. In truth the mooring was in a small inlet just off the river, not a large inlet but it gave enough protection from the winter weather to make it worth the hassle of getting my boat safely moored there. Keeping in mind that the river was actually an estuary, being able to get off the main flow of water over winter was a bonus.

Following a storm or prolonged period of rain, the waters became cluttered with debris washing down from up river. All kinds of items would tear down river carried by the strong winter currents. Discarded junk accompanied items lost overboard in the head long dash for the sea. Tree branches, car tyres, Mafia discards, loose boats of all varieties and tangles of rope joined with seaweed ripped from the river bed by the force of the winter current. I must point out that these items floated down river periodically, I did not mean for my description to resemble a stream of garbage travelling like a snake on the waters disturbed surface. In truth the free floating items of detritus appeared only following foul weather or a high spring tide and even then in very small numbers. However for those vessels still moored out on the main river, any one of these floating piles of rubbish could, and often did cause damage as they rushed on their way down river in the direction of the open ocean.

The fact that the river met the estuary also meant that occasionally the water could become quite rough, especially when wind over tide conditions prevailed. In these conditions, as the tide came in from the south, so the wind blew strongly from the north or visa versa. These events were made even worse during the spring tides, when the water rushed in or out against the wind. Remember the Teddy boy? White crested waves appeared on the water's surface and whipped the river into a frenzy of thrashing water. Attempting to venture out in conditions like this would be classed as reckless to say the least. Only the most foolhardy would venture out on the water on such days. I swear I once saw a swan trying to climb a tree to get away from the water, but I could be wrong. It is during these stormy conditions that other, larger debris flows down stream at a high rate of knots. Debris such as large branches and even tree trunks and the odd angler can shoot through the water like torpedoes and sink a vessel in the blink of an eye and without even an 'Excuse me!' Hulls made of plastic or wood cannot withstand such attacks and invariably gain large gaping holes and sink. Following a bout of bad weather, one would often see groups of people standing around a stricken vessel on the sandy river bed when the tide receded. I did not wish this fate to befall the Grumpy. Therefore despite the struggle, and the fact that my boat now stood on mud that could drag off any unsuspecting wellington boot, swallow mobile phones without trace and cover everything in an evil smelling and sticky black substance, I considered the effort worth while.

The area on which I moored the Grumpy over winter was quite secluded, a narrow inlet that dried out a few hours after high tide, with surrounding trees and a narrow lane that allowed access to the moored vessels. The lane itself sometimes flooded during a really high tide and on a number of occasions I had forgotten this fact and found myself stuck on board while my wellies floated away on the water. The water remained high for a couple of hours so I was forced to either continue the routine repair tasks or sit in the cold boat, swearing at the tide, the mud and my stupidity as I awaited the fall of the tide. If these little inconveniences were not bad enough, I would then have to climb down from the boat as soon as it dropped sufficiently and walk through wet mud and along the stony lane in only my socks. My wellies were by then happily on their way out to sea. Have you ever driven your car in bare feet and soaking wet trousers? Well I have and it is not a pleasant experience I can tell you. My wife was non too happy with the washing I presented her either. It always resulted in a clout round the ear before being ordered to go outside and hose off the excess mud and accompanying marine livestock from my clothes before going anywhere near the washing machine. Sometimes she even allowed me to remove the mud covered items of clothing before hosing them down with ice cold water!

Having the Grumpy moored beside the lane in a quiet spot had its advantages. I could, tide permitting, drive my car down the lane and park it within easy distance from my boat, thus forgoing the effort of carrying heavy tool boxes or crates of lager from the car park. I also discovered that having my car within such a close proximity to the water made me take more notice of the tides. I could stand the loss of another pair of wellies and an ear bashing from my wife, but I would certainly not risk my car becoming submerged under several feet of water. So my attention did not stray from the water level as I worked, or sat and partook of refreshment in the form of beer and crisps, whilst sat peacefully on the Grumpy. Other boats of all shapes and sizes were moored either side of me, I was on berth number thirteen out of fifty or sixty other berths so I regularly had company as other boat owners wandered past to or from their vessels. A hand full of these soon became friends and often we spent more time chatting than completing the work that all boats require over the winter months. The off season months passed quietly down on my mooring, the Grumpy was spruced up for the next season and I spent many enjoyable hours in the company of like minded souls, though as far as the wife was concerned, I was working very hard on repairs to the boat.

Nothing much happened that winter apart from one small accident that was entirely my fault. I kept my little tender on its own berth known as a frappe on the bank of the main river, I considered it safe enough from water bound missiles and other debris as it was on a drying bank and well out of the main current of the river. There was a low overhanging bank onto which my mooring line was attached, enabling my boat to be pulled up over the lower river bank by means of a rolling mooring. This is when the mooring line is looped; going from the anchoring bracket on land, out to weight sunken on the river bed and back again in one big circle. The boat was then secured to the rope. By pulling on one of the lines, the boat could be brought into shore while pulling the other line sent the boat out further into the water. This method was used by most of the tender or dinghy owners along the bank as it allowed the boats to float safely on the water while keeping them away from the bank until required.

On one particular occasion I had been to a family Christening. I was resplendent in my best suit, white shirt and tie as I greeted relatives and assorted family friends, gate crashers and passersby while partaking of alcoholic refreshment as one does. In fact I had quite a few alcoholic refreshments that day and to say my demure was happy might be something of an understatement. The day went well and soon came to an end, the family disappeared in all points of the compass, some to their homes, some off to continue the celebrations in a hostelry of their choosing and one I think was carted back to Her Majesties pleasure but I could not be certain. I had successfully avoided the chap in question all day, in truth his brutal appearance frightened the heck out of me, so when I saw two other men apparently escorting the chap to a waiting car, I naturally assumed he was being returned to prison, or a zoo. I was not certain which one was more appropriate.

For some strange reason known only to my ale addled brain, I decided I desperately need to check my little tender and the Grumpy as we left the Christening venue. I persuaded one of the few, or perhaps the only non drinker there to give me a lift. I certainly could not drive. I loath drink driving and anyway, I can never remember where the heck I parked my car! My non alcohol friend eyed me with suspicion at my request but I think he rightly anticipated an interesting outcome of my behaviour so finally agreed to drive me down to the river. On arrival I staggered from the car and made my way first to the river mooring of my tender. Once there I found the tide was in so I leaned out over the small bank and grasped one of the lines and pulled. Unfortunately things then went spectacularly wrong. First I leaned, or swayed too far out over the bank, and then I foolishly grasped the wrong line and pulled fiercely. Instead of the boat moving towards me over the full tidal water, I was met with resistance and as for every forward action there has to be an opposite reaction. The force of my pulling on the unmoving line caused me to over balance. And topple head first over the bank and into the water!

Suddenly I found myself submerged in the very cold water, just as suddenly I was no longer drunk as the water closed over my head and the seaweed began to hug me in its embrace. I swear I even saw a fish laughing at me. At first I panicked a little, I was not a strong swimmer and being dressed in my very best suit did nothing to ease my plight. Desperately I tried to remember how to swim. I thrust out with my arms and kicked out with my legs. My feet touched the bottom; I was in only three feet of water! Mentally cursing my panic and stupidity, I struggled to stand and scrabbled for a handhold on the lines in order to pull myself out. It was not going to be one of my best days as yet again I grasped the wrong line. This time it was the outgoing line, so with another splash I fell backwards into the river, receiving a mouthful of water as I had begun to swear loudly as I felt myself falling again. Spluttering and trying to stand in the slippery mud, I once more reached for a line. However my brain had now woken up and I wisely grasped both lines together. This time I was successful and I pulled myself up out of the freezing water, up onto the bank and flopped like a fish out of water on the grass surface. I lay there in a bewildered stupor for a moment or two as I gasped for air and shook with both cold and fright. After a moment or two of resuscitation, I staggered to my feet and went off dripping in search of my friend. I can only imagine what went through his mind when he saw this apparition in a soaking wet and muddy shirt, tie and best suit approaching his clean and tidy car.

As I neared his car, I got a distinct impression that he was not happy with the idea of a sopping wet and shivering wreck getting into his car. Without a word he climbed from his car, went round to the boot and removed two black plastic dustbin liners. Still silent he then gestured that I should strip off my wet clothes and put them in one of the black bags.

I looked at him in horror as I realised what he intended. By now I was very cold, miserable and - sober. 'I can't strip down here; we're in the middle of a car park!' I exclaimed in shock.

'It's either that or you walk home. Now get those soaking wet clothes off and put them in this bag.'

No relishing the long walk home I complied, though not without a few grumbles and mutterings. Luckily there where no other people in the car park when I began to remove my ruined best suit. But luck was not on my side that day. As soon as I removed my trousers, a gaggle of giggling girls came round the corner and into full view of my pathetic shivering figure standing in boxer shorts beside my friend's car. I had no where to run so I forced a cheeky smile on my face and gave them all a wave. After an all too long delay, mainly due to his hysterical laughter, my friend handed me the second black bag and instructed me to wrap it around my waist. With relief I obeyed, though I was not at all sure which did the most damage to my deflated ego, me standing in front of the girls in my wet boxers or me wrapped in a black bag. Once I was suitable, or not, dressed in my plastic skirt, my friend finally relented and allowed me into his car. Within moments we had left the still giggling girls and their very busy cameras behind and we were on our way home. I had no idea what my wife would say when she saw the state I was in and the bag containing a wet best suit, a once white shirt, two dripping socks and a shrivelled neck tie, but I was sure I would regret it. At least my friend turned the car heater on full for the journey home. I think my blue colour clashed with his car's upholstery.

Owning and sailing the Grumpy for some time, I had become quite good at handling the boat. I now often sailed solo out of the harbour but I still did not venture too far. Although we had the added safety of a National Coastwatch Institution lookout post positioned on a cliff top over looking the bay, I remained reluctant to put their skills to the test or to attempt the swim back to land. All my solo sailing trips were achieved within sight of the lookout and in the busiest section of the harbour mouth, least a passing vessel could come to my assistance if I did do something stupid. The Grumpy was not a fast boat, in fact as boats go, she would make a great flower trough. With her stubby keel and small sails she was more suited to sailing on lakes and rivers than the open sea. But I persevered and had many a good day pottering about on the water. My son James still accompanied me on occasion but now his school work was becoming more demanding so he had less time to mess about on the water with his accident prone father. With this in mind, I decided we should have some father and son time and experience something neither of us had done before. We would spend a night aboard the Grumpy.

Once the idea gained permission from the wife and mother, we set about organising the how's and when's. The decision was made, we would board the Grumpy late one afternoon when the tide was right, then sail down river to the harbour for a meal before returning to our mooring to spend the night. It really did sound a good idea at the time. The weather was warm and dry, the tides were at mid height so we would not be left standing on the sandy river bottom and the night was reported to be a clear one. On the designated day during the school holidays, we both set off to the river and our small adventure. I realise many, many people have stayed aboard a boat at night but the experience of sleeping while floating on the water would be a new one for us. Armed with sleeping bags, flasks of hot tea, a bottle of water, sandwiches and assorted snacks and my teddy bear we felt prepared for the night. My wife Joy hated the possibility of either of us getting hungry so our main baggage consisted of food. We also took torches, books and a small transistor radio, otherwise we were going to 'rough' it.

The afternoon passed in warm sunshine and a very slight breeze as James and I made our way to the harbour, tied up alongside a floating pontoon and visited one of the many eating establishments that appear to breed rapidly during the holiday season. After we had both eaten our fill plus a bit more just in case, we walked back to the boat in the growing dimness of the evening. The trip back to our mooring was uneventful, there was just enough light for us to find our berth and tie up for the night. I secured the little tender to one of the stern cleats, allowing it to wallow behind the Grumpy without it bumping into us and disturbing the hoped for peace of the night. Inside the cabin we laid out our sleeping bags on the berths under torchlight, drank a cup of tea, munched on a small snack and then settled down to a short read before sleep. So far all was going to plan. The berths were small and somewhat compact, but we were quite prepared for the squeeze. James of course did not care a jot; sleep was sleep no matter where he was.

Our toiletries consisted solely of the obligatory bucket and I prayed that the vast amount of food we had both consumed would not result in the need for a sit down job over night. I did have a toilet roll with me but alas, no air freshener and the close confines of the cabin would have not been conducive to privacy, or fresh air. The problem of urination was easily solved, there were billons of tons of water all around us, no one would notice a further few ounces if the need arose.

I switched off the small cabin light which was actually one of those stick on torch lights that one operated by pressing its surface, but it did the job and provided just enough light for us to organise ourselves for the night. With moments James was fast asleep, which did not surprise me. James had demonstrated on numerous occasions that he could sleep through virtually anything. I on the other hand, lay wide awake as thoughts and visions of every possible calamity that could befall us raced across my mind. What happened if the dinghy broke loose, what would we do if the mooring line broke and we drifted away as we slept? What if someone attempted to break in? What if we overslept and missed the tide, did we have enough supplies to wait out the return of the tide? These were just a few examples of the cheerful thoughts that denied my sleep that night. However none of the above happened and it was a far more natural event that awoke me some hours after I had finally gotten to sleep. It was my body that woke me, demanding that I answer a most urgent call, the call of nature. I was desperate for a pee!

Once my faculties had returned I realised this should present no problems as all I had to do was exit the cabin and, with my back against the wind, relieve myself as nature intended. The Pedro and the Senorita had plastic doors and when I say plastic when referring to parts of the boat, I mean GRP, glass reinforced plastic. The single door hung from a lip above the doorway and down across the entrance and could be secured when the vessel was not in use. However they were very cumbersome to use when one was staying aboard the vessel as one had to hang the door on the outside of the cabin from the inside, if that makes sense. A tricky task when one is fully awake and rational, much harder for a sleepy individual in the darkness of night upon a river.

I arose from my warm and comfortable sleeping bag and as quietly as I could, I stumbled, bashed my shins and stubbed my little toe on the way the door. I kept the cussing to a whisper but I need not have bothered, like I said, nothing wakes my son James. Only a short distance separated the sleeping area and the cabin entrance, possibly only a couple of feet, I cannot quite remember. Space had been made by the manufacturer for a tiny galley on the starboard side and a cramped toilet on the port side. Smart thinking really, as one could fry the bacon while sat on the loo. No, I never did that because I did not have a galley or a marine toilet aboard, but it would certainly be possible if I did. In too much of a hurry now, I moved to exit the cabin and stopped abruptly with a burst of choice words that I hoped my son did not hear. In my haste I had cracked my head on the top of the doorway. The blow almost caused me to fall backwards but with reflexes I did not know I had, I grabbed out and managed to catch a hold on the sides of the doorway. When the stars before my eyes cleared, I quietly removed the door and placed it to one side before carefully stepping out into the cockpit.

My need was bursting so in one leap I reached the gunnels, taking note of the wind direction before I unleashed my raging urge over the side. I realise many will be horrified to think in the twenty-first century, people still pee over board. However when one is out on the sea, or river or even deep in forests or moorlands, public conveniences tend to be slightly scarce. One only has to consider the amount of wild life out there happily going about their business without a care for human sanitation to realise what I had done was just a drop in the ocean! Anyway, my desperation relieved I finally had time to gaze about me. The night was clear and the stars twinkled above me. The black water lay calm beneath the boat and the world was quiet. Nary a seagull nor fornicating merpersons disturbed the peace. Street lights on the shore reflected across the water, creating silhouettes of the other vessels gently swaying on their moorings, and bathing those craft behind me in a pale yellow light. I stood there gazing out at the beautiful panorama that lay before me for long moments. A fox barking amongst the trees on the river bank to my rear abruptly brought me to my senses, and I realised I was beginning to freeze in the night air. I decided wisely to head back to the warmth of my sleeping bag.

I clambered in through the gangway once again before turning to replace the single plastic door. The door itself covered the vacant space between the warm cabin and the wide open night sky by simply hanging from a 'U' shaped channel attached across the top of the entrance like a cornice. Once hung in place and fitted tight against the bulkhead, the door could be secured via a padlock at its base. However when attempting to manhandle the door into position from inside the cabin, life became noticeably more difficult. The door, though only plastic, was quite solid and heavy and if one did not get the top lip of the door exactly in place within the cornice, the damn thing would simply fall off. Now please remember I was crouched in the cabin in almost total darkness, half asleep, cold and desperate not to wake my son. So hanging such a door in these conditions presented some unique problems. No matter how hard I tried, I could not get the door to hang correctly. I moved it from side to side and up and down but to no avail. I must have resembled a dog attempting to get through a three foot gateway with a five foot long branch held sideways in its jaws.

Finally my patience gave out. I manhandled the door into the cabin, no mean feat but I was getting annoyed now. Once inside I propped the door up against the cabin entrance and held it in place by jamming my boat hook hard against the inside door handle and the edge of my bunk area. Finally satisfied that the door would hold out the chill of the night and any rain that may fall, I returned to my sleeping bag to continue my nights rest. I glanced across at James and was pleased to see that none of my inept actions had woken him. My last thoughts concerned the security of the door, it may hold back the weather but it would certainly not obstruct any villain, nymphomaniac mermaid or even a rabid shrimp from gaining entry. I decided I did not care and went to sleep.

Daylight streaming through the cabin windows woke us both about six in the morning. The day appeared dry and sunny so we decided to make an early start. If we got back to shore in time, perhaps we could head somewhere for a fry up breakfast without my wife knowing. A fry up was definitely out of the question in our house. My wife insisted on grilling everything for health and waistline purposes, but surely the occasional deliciously fried breakfast would not hurt I thought, especially if she never discovered our dastardly deed. Firstly though, we had to vacate the cabin and get off the Grumpy. Almost as soon as James opened his eyes he spotted the propped up door on the inside of the cabin instead of outside where it should have been. I had hoped to awake early to remove the evidence but alas it was not the case. James peered at the door, and then his eyes went to the boat hook that was holding it in place before looking across at me with raised eyebrows.

'Why is the door in here?' he asked.

'I couldn't get it to fit last night so I propped it,' I replied shortly.

'Okay, so why did you take it down in the first place?'

'I needed some fresh air during the night, that's all,' I responded while climbing from my sleeping bag.

'Did you try putting it on the right way?'

James was now out of his own bag and examining the door as I replied, 'Of course I did! I could not get it to hang right and it was dark so I propped it up inside.'

'Did you try turning it the other way up?' he asked.

'No, it's supposed to go the same way up as it is now.'

'Dad? You do know the door is upside down don't you? It will never fit that way. The lip it hangs on is on the floor. The thing is upside down. How did it get that way?'

'I've no idea,' I shamefully replied, 'some how it must have been turned when I took it off. Still, no worries, we're up now so let's close up the boat and get some breakfast.'

Okay, I know I should have been more honest; however I did not wish to explain to my young son that I had been peeing in the river in the middle of the night. Of course James was intelligent and familiar enough with the out door life and the needs of our bodily functions. But nevertheless it did not feel right to admit his old man had been too sleepy or too daft to refit a simple door during the night, especially after warming a very small spot on the river. James refitted the door correctly, though not without a knowing glance in my direction that caused me to wonder if he knew more than he was admitting. That or he understood how clumsy and hasty or plain stupid I could be on frequent occasions. Pulling in the tender, we climbed aboard and headed back to shore for breakfast and I knew the perfect café. All in all the night had been very pleasant so we were both content with our little adventure. Yes I realise others have sailed around the world and spent months eating and sleeping aboard their boats, but to James and me it was a new experience. I daresay Dame Ellen MacArthur would wet herself laughing at our feeble attempts at seamanship, but everyone has to start somewhere. We never slept aboard again, there did not seem the need, we had done it and that was that. In truth it is only me that has never bothered again, James now fully grown has been on huge ships in many parts of the world. I still fall overboard from little boats on the river.

Sailing with the Grumpy continued over the years I owned the vessel and I enjoyed my time learning the skills of nautical pastimes. Some times I learnt a lesson, other times stupidity still got in the way, and on a very few occasions I even did something right. I ventured out of the harbour into the surrounding bay solo with little fear of my acquired sailing skills failing me. As I have said before, the Grumpy was an easy boat to sail, mainly because it was rather small and had too little sail area to break any speed records. I mostly had enough time to correct my mistakes and avoid drowning. On one particular day I had sailed out of the harbour and turned left or east if one wants to be correct. I seldom just sailed across the bay anymore; instead I explored the coastline surrounding the bay, enjoying the sensation of sailing to the best of my abilities. I pottered about sailing for a couple of hours in the warm sunshine and with a gentle breeze on my face. The Grumpy was handling well and I now owned a hand held marine radio so I could call for help if the worst did happen.

After some time I decided it was time to head back for my evening meal, my stomach was beginning to think my throat had been cut and was noisily making its emptiness known. I was positioned a safe distance from the cliffs off the shore so I simply turned the boat around and began to retrace my steps, if step is the right word for moving over water. Apart from my grumbling stomach I was quite content as I gazed at the nearby cliffs and the birds that flew about the rocky faces. I gazed for some time before I realised I had been staring at the very same section of cliff for some time. My sails were full and the water slid by my hull at a reasonable rate, a reasonable rate for the Grumpy that is. At first I worried that I was doing something wrong, I was sailing but not going anywhere. Suddenly I remembered a subject I had been taught while studying for my RYA certificate. I was experiencing the odd event of sailing over water but not over ground! That is to say the Grumpy was sailing happily along at the same speed as the tide was flowing towards us. So in effect although the water appeared to be moving past the boat, it was not actually moving over ground. I was virtually stationary. The tide was flowing under the boat at perhaps four knots while the Grumpy was also sailing at about four knots. However because I was heading into the direction of the tide, my boat was not making any headway at all.

What the heck was I to do I wondered, wait for the tide to turn or try and speed up the Grumpy. I decided I would attempt to get more speed out of my little boat and began adjusting the angle and tightness of the sails. Looking at the cliffs beside me, I saw I was actually moving, but I was now moving backwards! I had managed to unintentionally sail sideways in the Grumpy before, but now I was sailing backwards.

My actions had resulted in a reverse motion instead of the intended forward direction. Damn it! I did not want to use the little engine to get me out of trouble; surely I could figure this out. Luckily it was not too long before my brain woke up and I deduced that if I sailed to port and away from the cliffs, I might catch enough wind to power me and get out of the direct flow of the tide. I may just manage to get back into the harbour without the engine or screaming help to the rescue services. I swung my tiller and positioned the wind directly behind me and sailed at a run out towards the distant horizon. Running under sail is when the wind is blowing the boat forward, in other words the wind is blowing from behind the boat within roughly thirty degrees from either side of the stern. This is an effective method and allows the boat to capture the majority of available wind in its sails. When the wind is not exactly blowing from behind, it is referred to as a broad reach, and believe me, I was reaching as far as I could!

I sailed out about half a mile on a northwest course before making a wide turn until I was facing the harbour mouth. Now with the wind coming from my starboard side, I sailed on a starboard tack, obviously. I was astonished to discover my plan had worked and I was now sailing over both water and ground and making headway back to the security of the harbour and onto my mooring and home. The sails were full and the Grumpy leaned away from the wind and the water rushed past the hull. The Grumpy was making several knots, faster than walking or in fact swimming but I was in no danger of breaking speed limits. I did not care, it was one of those moments in time when all is right with the world, a moment remembered and often wished for again. I admit I was feeling quite pleased with myself, I had actually pondered a problem, come up with a solution and it had been successful.

What next I wondered, could I figure out the winning numbers on the Lottery? Perhaps not I sadly concluded.

Chapter Fourteen: Full Speed Ahead.

A tiny moment of sorrow squeaked in the back of my mind as I entered the harbour and the time came to lower the sails and motor back up river. The day had been a real sailing pleasure. I had not drowned which was always a good thing. The boat had not sunk which is handy for getting home for tea. I had not been attacked by any horny whales so it had been a good day and I was reluctant to let it stop. However time and tide waits for no man and it certainly was not going to wait for me. The harbour was reasonably quiet with just the odd few speeding tourists dashing around like insects in their midget rubber boats. There were not too many biannual sailors present, those convinced they knew more than they actually did. Neither was there an abundance of pompous semi naked boat owners, with their lily white skin glaring in the sunshine and bellies protruding out over their ridiculously patterned shorts. There was a distinct lack of bald heads covered with a little white cap emblazoned with a plastic anchor on its peak and perched at an angle that was considered daring – in the nineteen forties.

The usual number of small ferries scuttled across the water in their endless journey from one side of the river to the other, and woe betide any boat that got in their way. Water taxis vied for the business of ferrying people from their boats to the quay or to other individual destinations, helping passengers in high heels and broad rimmed hats transfer from boat to land with some degree of dignity, and that was just the men! Other working boats continued through their day, only noticing the odd bathing beauty posing on deck of the more expensive craft. Each beauty secretly hoping a rich man or a film director would notice them while in truth it was only the oily workers and fishermen that took time to observe them.

There were signs of other local pleasure sailors like me in the harbour. I could hear the clink of bottles and raucous singing drifting over the water from two particular vessels tied up at a sheltered pontoon near a small inlet. Other possibly more reserved or sober locals passed me going in or out of the harbour, each offering me a cheerful wave which I returned. I saw little of the larger fishing craft as I made my way through the harbour. Most of the fishing vessels would not be returning for a few hours yet, the fine weather meant many travelled that extra distance in search of the most profitable catch. Luckily for me, there were also no signs of the larger cargo carrying ships active in the harbour or any tugs. If I am honest, passing one of those huge vessels always frightened the heck out of me. I always felt like a massive steel wall was looming up to surround and engulf me in my tiny little plastic child's toy of a boat. Yes I know my boat was not a toy in the sense that a child could play with it in the bath, but against one of these mighty beasts, that was how I felt. Even the harbour master's vessels appeared to be having a respite from herding stray boats, Chinese junks and hordes of rampant day tripping canoes.

As I moved through the harbour I had passed several motor boats, speed boats and motor cruisers alike all enjoying the delights of our all too infrequent fine weather. Many were pulling skiers out into the bay on ski's that cut through the water like a knife before coming to an ignominious end in a flurry of water, floundering bodies and detached limbs. Others towed large rubber rings behind them with laughing people clinging on before they too suffered the same fate as the skiers. The larger motor cruisers simply powered through the water creating huge bow waves and leaving a frothy white wake as the skipper showed off his skills or lack of. These expensive boat owners never heard the profusion of profanities from smaller boat users that were left rocking dangerously in their wash. They were only concerned with showing off the boat to their passengers as they sipped assorted alcoholic beverages and lounged about on the luxurious upholstery aboard the vessels. I immediately became envious but shut the feeling from my mind. On that day at least, I was a very happy sailor. However, the images of skiers, lounging passengers and rubber rings flying across the water stuck in the deep recesses of my otherwise empty brain.

For that moment nonetheless, I was content to lower the sails on the little Grumpy and slowly motor back to my moorings in the warm sunshine of the day. I passed no one along the way once away from the harbour, nor did I meet any of my boating friends so the opportunity for a gathering of vessels followed by certain refreshments did not occur. A shame really because I was eager to relay my experiences of that day to who ever got close enough to be bored silly with my accounts of, in my opinion, my expert sailing. Alas no one, not even a lost mackerel or a confused cormorant ventured within hearing distance so I continued silently on up river. An hour or so later I had secured the Grumpy, stored the sails and made my way back to shore in the tender. I headed home to ear bash the wife, the kids, the dog and anyone else who dared to listen to the tale of my fantastic day.

Over a period of time the memories of those people messing about on the water in motorboats constantly surfaced in my mind. I spoke with James who was now at an age where he seldom accompanied me on my boating adventures, but I knew he would be keen on trying his hand at water skiing. Regrettably although keen, music, friends and of course girls were uppermost on his list of pastimes now but he dutifully listened to my thoughts and suggested I go ahead. Whether he agreed with my idea or simply wanted the old man to stop rabbiting I will probably never know, but I took him at his word anyway. I was to search for and attempt to purchase a motor cruiser that would be well outside my financial reach. However I would not let a little thing like money get in my way, providing I did not tell the missus of course. That would be risky, in fact it would be a dire threat to health and manhood if she discovered I intended getting a boat I could not afford.

As I have mentioned before, I think. I avoid getting into debt by bartering, swapping or part exchanging. I knew I would get a decent sized motor cruiser, the only question was how, and of course when? Obtaining a sleek, fast and show off vessel in my eighties, if I lived that long, would probably defeat the object somewhat. So to begin the process I began by letting all my boating friends and sailing associates know I was in the market for some form of motor powered vessel. Despite what many people may think, if one goes about it the right way, little is unobtainable. Of course a brand new sparkling gin palace was totally out of the question; however acquiring an older or disused vessel was certainly not. I spoke to my old friend John about the possibility of getting a motor cruiser and he appeared delighted. In truth he was now too old for sailing so the idea of boating by engine appealed to him. Once more John and I began a search for a suitable and of course, cheap vessel.

It was entirely by accident that I found the boat of my dreams. Well it was close enough to my dreams at least. Actually no, it was nothing like the boat of my dreams but it was near enough if one viewed it with an overdose of imagination and one eye closed. We had searched for several months but to no avail, all the boats offered to me were well outside my limited resources, I might as well have tried to acquire one of Richard Branson's infamous vessels. Not his hot air balloon I hastily add. But I continued anyway, the summer had long gone and my perfect day reduced to a distant memory. John and I visited many boat yards and spoke to any boat person we encountered. I spent many hours pouring over the Internet and boat adverts in the local papers, but it was much nearer to home where I discovered my new project.

By chance I was speaking to a boat repair and salvage bloke in the very hamlet from which I sailed regularly. He was an old man, well past his sell by date but his mind and abilities belied his age. The old man called Morris, was a small thin grey haired gentleman. He was renowned for having a very sharp eye for a deal. In fact I believe he would have been able to get money off from old Arkwright, a television character in the show, Open All Hours! So I approached cautiously, not wanting to be sold a non floating wreck or something that would cost me an arm and a leg to repair. However on that day, old Morris must have been in a generous mood. I had been passing the time of day with him as he was a likable chap despite his trading drawbacks, when I happened to mention I was looking for a motor boat. Quick as a flash his face lit up.

'I've got a boat that'll suit you lad,' he said as he grabbed me by the arm and began to lead me to where several boats were moored in a jumble beside his old shed.

I shook him off with a shrug and stated that I did not wish to buy one, I was rather hoping for a part exchange. His smile faded for a moment before returning again.

'You did say *part* exchange didn't you?' he queried.

'Yeah, I'm hoping to exchange the Grumpy rather than buy something outright,' I replied as he began tugging eagerly at my arm and leading me once more.

With a devious expression, Morris clarified as he pulled me along, 'Part exchange means you'll pay a bit of cash as well as swapping your boat doesn't it?'

This time I allowed him to lead me towards the assorted wrecks saying, 'Yep that's right, but I'm still not looking to pay much. Ideally I want something I can do up, or fix and repair. I'm not looking for a sparkling new boat, my mortgage won't stretch that far and my life would be at risk when the wife found out!'

'Oh, don't worry about affording it, I'm sure we can come to some agreement,' he concluded with a devious smile on his thin lips. I remained dubious. To be honest I felt like a small mouse under the black cold gaze of a snake. Not that Morris was evil or totally dishonest; he simply liked a fair trade, in his favour!

Arriving at the jumble of boats all proclaiming their readiness for sale via an assortment of hand painted signs adorned with the words, 'For Sale'. Morris pointed at one in particular. I admit I was immediately taken by the boat. I was careful not to show Morris my feelings, if I had I am sure the price would have increased by several percent immediately. The vessel Morris indicated was a cabin or motor cruiser exactly of the type I had been searching for. I guessed it was about nineteen foot long with a cabin and a large spacious cockpit. A forty horse power blue Volvo Penta engine rested on its stern and was controlled by levers attached on the starboard side of the inner freeboard near the cabin. A small steering wheel was situated on the cabin bulkhead itself, along with a fixed compass and brackets for other instruments which someone had obviously had away with one dark night. However because the boat was covered in green stuff, I did not know what it was, mould or algae or alien rust possibly, I had many doubts. Seeing my indecision, his salesmanship kicked in instantly and he assured me sincerely it would clean off easily. So why did I not believe him? My thoughts went back to the Passion Flower. That vessel also came in a delightful shade of mould. I climbed aboard the boat while retaining a poker face; I dare not let him know I was interested.

Inside the cabin was a sea toilet that looked complete on the port side, a two ring Belling gas cooker and a small stainless steel sink on the starboard side. Moving past this were two reasonably sized bunks with storage room beneath them. A triangular berth only suitable for a small child or a dog at the bow just in front of the anchor locker completed the interior arrangements. Shelving reached along each side of the cabin, resting about two foot above the bunks and a tiny access hole through a wooden bulk head in the bow of the cabin allowed one to reach the anchor, anchor tube and storage locker.

Out in the cockpit, the space was amazing. Usually a cockpit is cramped with seating and storage units, but here there were none except a fold down seat in front of the steering wheel. There was one seat at the stern, under which all the steering cables were situated. The front part of the seat was covered with a small door enclosing a storage compartment, but the sections on each side were open to allow access to the cables. A space for the battery and fuel tank lay behind the door in the compartment situated in the middle. Neither of us knew what make the boat was, however while leaning over the stern to check the engine mounts, I had found a small plaque attached to the stern that stated the words, *Stuart Stevens of Liverpool* on it, but no other information. Nonetheless it appeared to be a good boat and I was unsure why Morris wanted to sell it or the price he would ask. I did not discover the design name until many years later when I happened to see one on the Internet.

My prospective purchase was a Stuart Stevens Weekender. Just under nineteen foot long with a six foot three inch beam, nice and wide I thought, it had a draft of approximately one foot and was obviously constructed of GRP. The hull screamed speed, a deep 'V' shape that flowed back towards the stern. The freeboard curved back from the bow in a majestic sweep before edging up slightly towards the stern. In my opinion, the lines of the boat were beautiful, very similar to a Shetland 535 but much more curvy and without the straight edges and angles of the Shetland. The Weekender certainly impressed me but it was not me that needed convincing, it was the wife. I did not wish to be reminded of my mistake for the rest of my life, especially following those infamous words,

'What's wrong with you?' I would ask like any concerned and dutiful husband.

'Nothing!' would be her snapped reply.

Oh hell, no man should suffer the threat that single word could insinuate with such enormous proportions that could last an eternity. So I took great care in reaching a decision that in truth, I had already made.

My examination of the boat complete, both Morris and I stood on the mud beside the boat and the business of haggling began. I stated that I was not considering buying the boat outright; it had to be a part exchange for the Grumpy. Morris of course only wanted cash but soon realised I was not going to budge. Then the question concerning the value of the Grumpy arose. I had a figure in mind but as expected Morris suggested a much lower sum and so the haggling continued. Morris was a mean and devious haggler and several times I had to fight hard not to end up buying the boat, his house and his wife! He did refuse to sell me his dog though. In an attempt to gain a respite and lick my wounds, I asked why he was not selling the Weekender himself and in a moment of weakness, Morris let slip some information that I could and would use against his price. Firstly the boat was almost totally covered in a green substance, it was mud splattered and very dirty. More importantly and much more costly, all the windows were crazed and opaque with moss growing everywhere. Leaves littered the decks and had even found their way into the cabin. Seagulls obviously loved this floating public convenience and small boys had used the boat as a target to improve their stone throwing skills. Morris admitted that he would have trouble selling it to any other unsuspecting customer without quite a lot of work being done first. He simply could not be bothered. He knew that I did not mind fixing and repairing boats and I did not require a vessel that gleamed in the sunshine and was immediately sea worthy. I was an idea customer for a tired and forlorn boat that no one else wanted.

At last the deal was struck and following a brief handshake I became the owner of a green, tired and dirty Stuart Stevens Weekender. What had I done I asked myself repeatedly as I drove home to inform the family. What would old John think of my latest acquisition? Anyway, it was too late, I had sold the Grumpy and bought the Weekender. Once I returned home, I phoned John following a tide of apathy from the family but he at least, appeared pleased. I think he was simply bored and any excuse to get his hands dirty again was fine by him. We arranged to join up beside the river so he could have a proper look that afternoon, and following a brief lunch, I set off to meet him.

There we stood in the mud, two men in wellies staring at a dilapidated green boat, the origin of which I had no idea at that time remember. I went to scratch my head, remembering too late that my hands were already covered in the sticky black mud of the river inlet.

Morris had kindly undertaken the exchange while I was home having lunch. He had removed the Grumpy from my mooring and manoeuvred the Weekender in its place. Most likely he was ensuring I could not go back on the deal. The Grumpy was clean, sea worthy and ready to go and the odds of a sale had greatly increased in his favour. Secured in my winter mooring sat my new acquisition in all its forsaken glory, awaiting the tender care of a pair of enthusiastic idiots or the indignation of the boat scrap yard, not much of a choice really. I allowed John to clamber in and out and under the boat while I took a closer look at the vessel. I had thought to bring a bucket and a cloth with me, and in a moment of madness I filled the bucket with river water, wetted the cloth and began to scrub at a patch of hull. To my utter surprise the green quickly disappeared and the real colour of the boat was revealed. It was white, or at least it had once been white but now it was a sort of off white cream, if that makes sense? Anyway, I mentioned madness earlier because once one began clean, the compulsion to continue takes over. I could not leave just one small patch of clean hull; hence I ended up cleaning the entire starboard section of freeboard while John continued to potter and mumble.

We checked the boat over thoroughly and decided that maybe, just maybe I had done a good deal. The vessel was sound, most things on it worked and it was water tight, a fact made evident by the amount of rain water contained within the craft. There was a pipe fitted that suggested it had once been attached to a bilge pump, but alas that too had gone to the big boot sale in the sky. So after the exertion of cleaning, I then set about pumping out the water with a hand held bilge pump. It was not long before my sweat was adding to the water level inside the boat. Once the small lake had been bailed out, we found the cabin floor and examined the numerous items of flotsam and jetsam that littered the cabin space. Finding nothing of real interest like golden doubloons or treasure maps, we moved out and clambered onto the narrow side sections that I think are called the side decks, just inside the gunwales. Holding on tightly to the coach roof hand rails, I did not want to land on my backside in the mud again, we examined the windows and concluded the best thing to do was renew them completely. A decision easier said than done as it turned out. Earlier while inside the cabin we had found a blue canvas canopy and the frame on which it fitted, so in order to keep leaves, rain and wild animals out, we erected the thing as best we could. Neither of us had any idea how the canopy fitted but we got it up and hoped that the wind would not whisk it away. Finally after some cleaning, erecting the canopy and much discussion, both John and I agreed we were delighted with my new toy.

The boat had several other fittings that I have not yet mentioned. Around the bow was a stainless steel hand rail which, I decided, would come in very handy in keeping me from falling overboard, not that I tend to be accident prone of course. It is just that I do have lots of accidents, and falling overboard would be very easy for someone like me. Mounted on the cabin or coach roof, which ever description is correct, was a four section wind screen, the front being split in two panes with another pane set at right angles on each side and all were set in an aluminium frame. The frame appeared to be in reasonable condition but seeing through the wind screen itself would take Superman's X-ray vision. Another item that would need replacing I noted with a sigh. In the centre of the roof a tall fibreglass aerial indicated the once presence of a marine radio, of course there was no sign of it now. A small mast with one white light stood about two foot high and the aerial was bracketed to it. Navigation lights were attached to either side of the cabin structure with two small handrails to which we clung desperately to while closely examining the cabin windows. There was one window on each side and a forward large screen. The hand rails ran along the edges of the roof above the windows. Around the side decks, a rubbing strip constructed of wood ran the entire length of the boat. Cleats were situated two at the bow, one mid way on each side and two more at the stern to provide anchorage for mooring lines. Or for hanging plastic bags full of lager cans in the water to keep cool I concluded. It was just a matter of priorities. A larger bollard cleat stood central on the bow deck along with a ninety degree angled aluminium pipe that fed the anchor chain from the locker below out onto the deck. I have no idea what this is called either but I am sure you will.

Inside the cabin some nice thoughtful person had fitted curtains to the windows. Pointless now as the windows were in such bad condition that one could not see through them anyway. Privacy was assured with or without the tattered curtains and I decided they would certainly have to go. They reminded me of those garish patterns popular in the nineteen sixties. The companion way into the cabin was secured by a folding wooden door but whether this was original I had no way of knowing. The door was hinged down its centre and folded back on the opposite side to the driving seat and wheel. Moving back inside once more, there was no method to our search, we were simply clambering over the boat like hyperactive monkeys. Below deck we found all manner of ropes, fenders, wiring and assorted detritus that one gathers in a boat, just in case something was ever needed, but never is. And finally a folding anchor and nine foot of chain were attached to a coiled rope, the length of which I did not know lay in the anchor section of the bow. I was certainly not going to uncoil it just to find out. After an hour of poking, pulling, lifting and examining, John and I made a list of things that were needed in order of priority. Top of the list was written in bold was, head for the pub, have a pint and then discuss what needed to be done.

Chapter Fifteen: Gin palace or Beer Bucket?

Over the next few weeks I spent many happy hours in solitude beside the river cleaning and scrubbing the boat. Yes I realise that sounds very strange, enjoying cleaning a green and muddy boat but the peace and quiet of the little inlet was a haven from all the cares of the world, and of course the chores at home. With the boat covered in green and dark brown mud, one could say it was camouflaged and once or twice I did lose the damn thing because I could not see it! But as the green and brown gradually became white, finding it became easier. I had not yet come up with a name for the vessel but I was sure I would arrive at one soon. Although I will admit that on occasion when the green stains refused to budge, I did come up with a selection of choice names for the boat. At the time, with my arms red from water and cleaning fluids and my legs and feet cold from standing in the black mud, any name I came up with would have been either derogatory or offensive.

Being honest I did enjoy the odd era or two of cleaning because it allowed me to get an in depth opinion of the boat, and all in all I was happy. I could image myself clothed in the style of a wealthy yacht owner, with the decks littered with beauties in bathing suits while moored in Monaco and watching a Grand Prix. I dreamed of days spent with water skiers bouncing over the waves behind me, of gin fuelled parties aboard while dressed in blazer and white flannels. Pretty stupid I know, but ones mind wanders far when engrossed in hour upon hour of scrubbing a hull, desks and superstructure of a boat. Plus of course I would not have gotten many bathing beauties on such a small boat, two or three perhaps but I am not greedy, two or three would do nicely, providing the wife did not find out.

Soon or not so soon depending how one viewed a time scale, the boat almost looked new once more. All the metal work had been polished, all surfaces cleaned, the cabin was fit for habitation again and even the sink had been unblocked and the toilet sparkled. Now came the time to examine and repair such nautical delights as the compass, all the wiring for the navigation and cabin lights, the steering cables and any other such modern piece of equipment that was attached to the boat. I did discover while cleaning the barnacles and fish tails from the bottom that at one time some form of speed indicator or knots per hour thing was fitted to the bottom. How it worked, if it worked and what it actually did was alien to me so I sought help. Not from John this time as one needed to slither under the boat, so for this reason I called upon my friend Don. He knew all about the wizardry otherwise known as nautical equipment and he was still young enough, just, to climb under the hull. Don informed me with great patience that the flappy thing was in fact a boat speed log impellor that had been inserted in the hull beneath the boat. The impellor measures the speed and distance the boat is travelling over water and is calculated by an electrical instrument on deck known as the Log. This then enables the boat skipper to obtain a visual figure of that speed. It is a very useful and often necessary piece of equipment for navigation. So far, my boating experience had not required the knowledge of speed over water, as far as I was concerned, I was either moving or not moving. Or in the case of the Grumpy, which way was I moving!

I personally wondered why anyone would deliberately make a hole in the bottom of a boat but Don assured me it would not leak, and if it did, one simply replaced it. That is all well and good I thought, but what happens if it leaks while out at sea? Okay so I was new to this modern boating equipment game, all I had needed were sails, two oars and a Seagull outboard which occasionally worked.

With Don's help and instruction, I traced to wires back to where there should have been some form of instrument that would show what speed the boat was doing. I found where the wires lead but there only remained an empty space now. Those light fingered buggers had half inched that as well. While Don was under the boat, he called out that I would need to replace the anode sometime soon. I enquired what the heck an anode was and received numerous tut, tut's before getting an answer.

In a calm voice delivered with an obvious undertone that I was a nautical moron. Don explained what an anode was and what it did. Remember he had just finished informing me about impellors and logs, no wonder he thought I was an idiot.

'A hull anode helps protect your engine propeller against corrosion from being constantly submerged in the water. It is often called a sacrificial anode because its purpose is to lose its own substance and corrode to save you having to keep replacing propellers.'

'Oh,' was my witless reply. I now know an anode is necessary to protect the propeller and any other metal objects that may be dangling in the water, I know a chemical and electrical reaction takes place, but that is the limit of my understanding.

I made full use of Don while he was there, getting him to check the boat over as he was far more experienced and knowledgeable than John or me. He happily, well almost happily agreed and began pointing out little things that would require attention, often having to explain to me what they were and what they actually did. My standing as a moron grew steadily that day. However I now had a clear picture of what I needed to do to make the boat seaworthy. To be honest I was surprised at how little it required, the boat was in fair condition and apart from the odd piece of equipment or fitting that had found its way into some thieving individual's pocket, much of the tasks to be done were superficial.

The windows were the biggest chore that required action, not quite as important as the hull in the overall safety of the vessel, but it does help if one can see out whilst sipping a gin and tonic in the cabin amidst those imaginary bathing beauties. Another minor reason for having windows in good condition was to stop large waves crashing on to the boat and shattering windows on its way into the cabin and filling the boat with water. Not really an ideal situation to have a boat full of water, it tends not to float too well in those conditions. Before he went, Don gave me some advice on the material to use when replacing the windows. I was grateful as I did not have a clue and I do not think John would have known either. The windows appeared to me as some form of Perspex and that was the height of my knowledge. However when I visited a plastics retailer, I was informed I would need a material that would withstand the ultra violet rays of the sun. As I was repairing the vessel during the winter months, the possibility of sun damage did not occur to me. The retailer told me I would need a type of external acrylic, I replied I would consider his suggestion and ran off to Google the word, acrylic.

After reading many long words on the subject of acrylic, I headed back to the retailer to purchase some. Now I had a strong heart in those days but when he mentioned the price it nearly killed me!

Unfortunately it appeared if I wanted to do a good job, I would have to pay. With tears running down my cheeks I ordered a sheet of this *poly(methyl 2-methylpropanoate)* or acrylic to us ordinary folk and paid the cost, wondering if the boat was really worth such extravagance. The sheet came in sizes of eight foot by four foot, the normal size of a sheet of plywood, but a damn sight more expensive. But like a true boatman I paid the cost and went home for a cry while I awaited delivery.

Old John agreed to help me cut, shape and replace the windows and it was provident that he did, left to myself the resulting bodge would have been a disaster. John was meticulous in his measuring so I left him that chore. Because the sheet was too big to manhandle and cut by the waters edge, we used his drawings and measurements to cut out all the windows at my house before transporting them down to the boat. Cutting acrylic was a chore in itself, as the jigsaw cut through the material, so it welded itself closed again behind the hot blade. After a period of cussing, stamping feet and shouting at the neat welded lines, we discovered that by covering the line to be cut with masking tape, it stopped the acrylic rejoining itself.

Finally all the windows were cut and shaped and ready to be fitted. Hah! Such an easy task we thought, we were disillusioned quickly.

Obviously our first task was to remove all the old and crazed windows from the boat, and this proved to be somewhat difficult. It rapidly became apparent that a previous owner of the said vessel had replaced the windows once before, unfortunately he or she or most likely it, had used mild steel nuts and bolts. All the damn things had rusted and would not undo. So I brought forth my favourite and most used tool, a hammer. Using a hammer and a cold chisel we bashed off each nut and pushed out each bolt. To say the air was blue at the previous idiot's expense would be an understatement. Using a chisel in a plastic boat is not advised under normal circumstances but we had no choice. I was inside the cabin belting each nut with gusto, but cold hands and cramped conditions meant my fingers suffered profusely during that period. At the end of the day I had so many cuts and bruises on my hands and fingers that I could barely lift a pint of beer to my lips, but I managed.

Once all the windows were out, we began fitting the new. I thanked God, Mohammed and

Buddha and any other deity that may listen for the simple invention of the cordless drill that day. Drilling new holes with a hand drill in the hard glass reinforced plastic would have been a chore too far for my sore hands. It took a couple of days to seal each window with a ribbon of silicon before bolting them in place with new stainless steel nuts and bolts. But when the job was done, both John and I agreed it was worth it, the boat suddenly looked like a boat should. A clean hull and superstructure and new windows improved the appearance of the boat noticeably, and more importantly I thought, it improved its value.

Now all that was required was the windscreen and I undertook that job myself. Strangely it did not take long and went almost without a single hitch, I say almost because there were indeed several hitch's but in a true manly manner I coped. I will admit the ability to see where one is heading on the water is a distinct advantage to ones well being, and that of the boat of course. Finally I had all round visibility, from on deck at the controls, to inside the cabin. So what was the second item I decided that day? Curtains! I would need curtains because the good visibility worked both ways. Yes I know I was derisive toward the curtains already on the boat when I first purchased it. But now with clear visibility both in and out of the boat, I decided I needed my privacy. Following bribes, lies and many compliments, I wheedled my way into the wife's good books and persuaded her to make me some curtains. As a result, for the next week I was busy completing all the overdue chores at home. A high price for curtains I know, but these things have to be done and I did end up with a full set of matching curtains as a reward for all my efforts. Plain blue curtains I will stress, not flowery patterned ones left over from a sixties hippie pad.

Now the boat was ready, there was only one thing left to sort out. I spent a few moments trying to remember what that was as I gazed lovingly at the shining vessel before me. I had still not remembered when a friend happened along and jogged my memory.

'Boats looking good mate, when are you actually taking it out on the river? I assume the engine is good, you'll need a good engine to push that boat through the water,' he commented as he stood examining my new pride and joy.

Realisation struck with a thump but I quickly hide my embarrassment and boldly replied as confidently as I could, 'Yep, 'course the engine is ready. Only a mug would leave that till last, after all a boat's no use without an engine, is it?' I lied with indignation.

'Tis true, a boat with out 'er motor is just a bathtub. Glad you've got it all sorted. Any chance of a fishing trip when it's out on the river?' queried the friend who was rapidly becoming just an acquaintance.

'Yeah sure, anytime,' I responded, lying again of course, 'just give me a bell when you want to go out fishing.'

'Will do. See ya later,' he replied as he walked off to annoy some other poor person who owned a boat, because he did not.

The engine! I had totally forgotten that the engine may and most probably would need some attention. Going by the condition of the boat when I obtained it, I would be lucky if the engine worked at all. It was time to phone a friend. Luckily I knew a man who was a dab hand with engines but first I thought I would take a look at the beast myself. I have never owned such a huge powerful engine before, a forty horse powered Volvo Penta is only slightly different to a four horse power British Seagull – isn't it? I did know something about engines and I was curious to see what was under the cover anyway. Releasing the catches and pulling off the blue engine cowling, I received a shock. The engine appeared clean and with no rust, no corrosion and even the spark plugs gleamed! I had expected the worst, very much worse if my previous experience was anything to go by, but not this time. Hoping the engine was in neutral I reached for the pull starter cord and gave it a yank. A big mistake! The damn thing did not move and I nearly tore my arm from its socket. Unluckily with every action there is a reaction, something I was becoming very familiar with now. So when the force I used to pull the cord resulted in no backward movement, I was very nearly thrown forward clear over the stern. Regaining my balance and rubbing my sore arm at the shoulder, some intelligence crept into my brain and I realised that pulling over a forty horse power engine might just require more effort that a lowly Seagull outboard. This time I used both my shaky hands and placed one foot against the transom for additional support when I pulled the starter cord. My efforts were rewarded as the engine turned over without a squeak, groan, rasp or clang. This also proved the engine was not in gear, much to my relief. In my haste to pull over the engine, I had not actually checked if it was in neutral. I was satisfied with the result even though I obviously could not start the thing up at that moment. For one I had no fuel on me, and as the boat was now sitting on the muddy river back, I deemed it somewhat unwise to start a forty horse engine propeller turning into a huge mud whisk.

Following a quick trip back to my car for the appropriate tools, I pulled out each plug and cleaned them before moving on through the engine. I was still amazed by the condition and I could hardly contain my eagerness to fire the Volvo Penta up. Alas that would have to wait so once I finished with the engine and replaced the cowling, I moved on to the controls that were situated on the starboard side of the companion way. Twin cables ran from the engine, along under the gunwale up to the control box. The control box consisted of two levers, one being a throttle while the other manipulated the gears, forward, neutral and reverse. An ignition key socket was located on the front of the box but I discovered it was not connected to the engine. As the engine did not possess an electric starter motor, I gave the ignition switch no more consideration. Grasping the throttle lever, I worked it backwards and forwards to check its movement and all seemed fine. Next I reached for the gear level and went to move it forward. Ah ha! Here we go I thought as the lever refused to move, where's my hammer? I have always found a hammer to be most useful when something did not move. It was the first tool I reached for, no spanner or screwdriver reached my hand until I had given the offending object a good bashing with the hammer. Sadly the magic tool failed me on this occasion so I was forced to examine the control box and gear lever closer, wondering if I would need a bigger hammer.

An hour or so of swearing, greasing, swearing, manipulating and even more swearing, I eventually freed one of the linkages that proved to be the cause of the seizure. Once that was done the gear lever worked properly and I could see that the position of the control box lever was transferred to the small protruding gear connection on the engine. Next came the steering and the twin steering cables ran from the steering wheel and alongside the control cables beneath the gunwale. All seemed fine with the mechanism but again I could not be totally sure until the boat floated once again on the incoming tide. With the propeller stuck firmly in the mud, it obviously rebuffed any efforts I made to turn the engine, so I gave up and decided to wait for water. Just then I received another visitor, it was the same bloke from earlier returning along the bank to his car. Just the person I wanted to see twice in one day, twice in a life time would have been enough!

'Seen you pullin' that thing, didn't expect it to be so 'ard I noticed. How's yer arm?' grinned the one time friend.

'Just forgot that's all,' I replied in a bit of a huff, 'I intended checking the engine over today but I know it works fine. Once there's enough water it'll be fine.'

'Never had it runnin' 'ave ee? Come on, own up,' he shouted across to me while I simply wished I owned a gun.

'Well not personally but Morris said it runs fine.'

'Ee don't believe that Morris do ee? Can't never tell with ee, bet it don't work!' sniggered my no longer friend before he turning his back on me and continuing on his way, chuckling to himself as he went.

In return I muttered a number of obscenities at his back, mainly regarding cement boots and fish food.

He did not hear or choose not to, I could not be sure. I continued that day gradually working through the boat checking and fiddling with what worked and what did not and was pleased to discover that most things in fact did work. Or at least appeared as if they would work when actually put to the test.

The subject of a name for my boat niggled at my mind throughout the day. I had found a name plate in one of the cabin lockers that may have belonged to the boat but I decided not to use it. Even I would not give any boat such a stupid name. I did not know who the previous owner or owners were, but who ever had named the boat was most certainly a cretin. I mean, who in their right mind would name a boat, the Manic Destroyer? What kind of name was that? What could be threatening about a nineteen foot motor cruiser designed for pleasure weekends on the water? I have known boats to be given male testosterone names before but at least they were all huge muscle vessels, not a small pleasure craft. I decided there and then I would give serious thought to a name for my new boat, I did not know what name at that time but I would think of something, I hoped.

I gave quite a lot of thought to naming the boat over the next weeks and on into months as winter departed and the cold rain and grey skies of spring arrived. Should I give it a romantic name, Sunset Rose perhaps? Or Camouflage in memory of the state I found the boat in. Perhaps I should call it the Gin Palace as that is how I wanted to envision it. However let's be honest, Beer Belly could have been the more appropriate name. Strangely when I bounced these suggestions off my family, the response was less than enthusiastic, even down right apathetic. I did not receive the loud applause I expected at such a clever selection of possible names, I could not understand the reaction, I thought my choices were great. Strangely I wished to please the family and I fully admit that their common sense was much more reliable than mine. Finally and with the consent of family, friends, pub regulars, wandering musicians and my dog, the name decided upon was - Mon Bateau! Hah, now that has confused a few of you I bet. But consider who had to come up with a name for my boat? Remember who had worked hard on my boat, all the dreams I held for my boat, the pride I felt in my boat. So I simply called my boat, 'My Boat' but to be a bit classy I used the French language, the chosen name was, Mon Bateau which means *My Boat* in French. Clever huh? Well it certainly confused the locals and frightened the heck out of the resident wildlife, especially the frogs . . . .

Chapter Sixteen: Mon Bateau

Okay I do not speak French, I did attend classes in French at school but it was all foreign to me. I did not learn much but I can speak a few choice French words, least that is what I tell my kids when a foreign word slips out. I did consider naming my boat in Cornish, but I do not speak that either. So my boat was now named Mon Bateau and it was ready to go. One fine spring morning, one of the few that year, John and I set out for a test run and to move the boat onto its summer mooring on the river. All went well surprisingly. I did not even pull my arm from its socket when starting the engine, always a good start to the day I thought. I had started and tested the Volvo Penta occasionally on the winter mooring, when the tide had reached high enough for the boat to float and the fish get out of the way. It had started reasonably easy, though I now had muscles in my arms that I did not have before. The engine had been run for an hour on a couple of occasions, just idling away by itself while I waited to discover any problems that arose as the motor warmed up. There were none, the Volvo chugged away happily and filled me with confidence, a feeling I was not entirely comfortable with.

We gently manoeuvred Mon Bateau out from its winter berth and onto the wide river by keeping the big Volvo Penta almost on tick over alone. My pride soared as the sparkling clean and shiny vessel knifed through the water under the gaze of several locals and tourists, who had risked our temperamental spring weather to take an early holiday. As the boat was performing so well, John and I agreed we should give it a run before mooring. We were not far from the shore when we reached that decision, having made a right turn out of the small inlet. I pointed the bow down river and opened the throttle to its full extent. With a roar the boat surged forward, I had again forgotten a forty horse power engine is a tad more powerful than a four horse Seagull. With a further push on the throttle the bow came up and the resulting wake frothed furiously behind the craft as it quickly picked up speed. For those who may not know, a wake in boating terms is a track of disturbance in the water that resembles turbulent waves spreading out in a huge V shape from the stern of a boat. The faster the boat travels, the bigger the wake behind it. These wakes can be a real nuisance when a large vessel passes as the resulting wave will rock the heck out of any smaller craft attempting to cross that section of water. Many a tiny boat has suffered the indignity of being over turned by the waves from a large wake hitting them broadside. Knowledgeable boaters understand this little detail and as soon as a gin palace or weekend sailor ventures near travelling too fast, will point their bow into the oncoming shock of waves and thus avoid an early bath.

The wake from a fast moving vessel can also present problems on the shoreline; hence the necessity for speed limits on rivers and estuaries. Waves from a wake will hit the shore and hasten the erosion effects, washing banks away which in turn help silt up the waterways. Another effect is that those same waves, smaller than a tsunami I admit, but still a force to be reckoned with will eventually wear down even the strongest water side structure such as walls and pathways and will create havoc with other moored vessels in the vicinity. There is one further problem with a high wake hitting the shore but this is often classed as a kind of devilish sport for the locals. I was to unwittingly partake in that questionable sport now.

Down river we shot, I had steered too close to the slipway in my haste to feel the power and I had not given any thought to the size of the wash streaming from the stern. All too soon but alas too late I remembered when I glanced behind me and saw to my horror, and no little humour, that my wake had hit the slipway and gushed up and over it like a huge wave hitting a sea wall in a storm. The resulting wave reared up over the slipway and soaked all those people who stood on its edge watching us motor past. Locals and tourists combined scattered in their flight to avoid the water and seaweed that showered over them in a cold and dirty deluge. Small fish, the odd lost crocodile and a nude mermaid flapped in desperation at the feet of those caught too close to the edge. Watching the reactions of those who now regretted their proximity to the waters edge, I felt a slight pang of guilt. Oh heck! I am going to have to supply a lot of beer later, to calm those who were now dripping wet and shaking fists at me. Luckily over the roar of the engine I could not hear what they were shouting, but from their expressions I gathered they were not shouting words of encouragement. Quickly I pulled back the throttle and slowed the boat down, I was heading towards an area which held many other moored vessels and I did not want their owners cursing me as well. And of course there was the little matter of the harbour patrol, the speed limit on the river was six knots and I had no wish to obtain the dubious distinction of getting a fine for speeding on water!

Leaving the small hamlet and the wet spectators behind, I sailed the Mon Bateau at a more sedate pace down river towards the harbour. I say sedate but in truth it was the fastest I had ever made that journey before, even with the throttle virtually closed. I tried not to think of those poor wet souls behind me but I endeavoured. I stood proudly at the helm, waving at other boat owners that I passed on route, even those craft much bigger and more expensive than mine. I felt the vessel I now owned matched any that came near me that day. Of course they did not, some were smaller, and many were simple fishing dinghies but several were sleek powerful and beautiful examples of modern marine pleasure craft. I did not care a hoot though, in my mind I was on a magnificent motor cruiser. As we neared the harbour and the open sea, I was filled with expectation at the prospect of speed on the open water. Once we reached the harbour,

I was surprised to notice just how many other craft got out of my way. They had hardly noticed me in either of my sail boats or the Passion Flower, but now most vessels scattered before me and I soon found myself on the open sea. I assumed the appearance and power of the Mon Bateau gave the impression I was a rich man playing with his toy and considered as a hazard to health on the water. No one would have kept away from me if they realised I was a boating peasant, least that is what I concluded anyway. I could not in all honesty claim the presence of Mon Bateau frightened anyone. It had to be the impression that I was one of those inexperienced sailors with more money than sense that caused other craft to hurriedly avoid me. Either way I did not care, with John sat dozing at the stern and the engine purring nicely, I continued out from the harbour mouth with a serene soul. Surely it could not last.

Once I was clear of any other vessels and away from the imposed speed limit, I let the engine rip, full throttle out across the waves. Spray quickly soared over the bow and the wind caused by our speed through the water blew it back onto my face. I smiled in contentment, until a shout from behind me interrupted my pleasure.

'What in heaven's name are you doing? You could have warned me!' shouted an irate John as he wiped water from his face.

'Sorry John, were you asleep?' I asked innocently.

'Yes I flaming well was! I didn't expect to be woken by a sea water shower. What's the hurry anyway? Not thinking of a day out in France are you? Don't think your wife would be too happy about that, you going without her that is!'

By now John had joined me at the helm and despite his angry tone; I could see he too was thrilled at the boat's power and ability on the sea. Yes I realise the Mon Bateau was nothing special and was not hugely powered, but on that day and following the years of sedately moving under sail or being propelled by small engines, the speed and manoeuvrability of the Mon Bateau felt like a Formula One race car. Seeing his face I gestured that John should take a turn at the helm and he happily took my place and grasped the wheel. Suddenly I was thrown backwards as he pushed the throttle even further forward. Now we were skimming over the water faster than I had ever sailed before. I admit that speed on a sailing yacht is always negotiable with the wind, but having the power at ones finger tips was indeed enthralling. I could barely see over the cabin roof as the bow reared up to the blue sky and the Volvo Penta loosened its muscles as we roared over the waves.

'So where are you off too then?' I shouted over the screaming engine and rushing slipstream, 'Spain by any chance? At this rate we'll be there in a minute or two. Thought you didn't like the boat going so fast?' I knew John was a fan of Spain and had visited there several times.

'Nope, I quite like the speed; it was being woken up with a cold shower that I didn't appreciate. Anyway, what better way to test the boat and its engine? I want to see what it will do just as much as you do.'

'Okay let's see, but try not to mow down any smaller boats or ram a cargo ship will you?' I pleaded.

'Ha don't worry, I'll be careful, more careful than you would be I expect. Right, which way do you want to go? West to the next harbour or east and see what's there?' responded John as he steered the vessel off to the west before I could reply.

'I guess we're going this way then?' I enquired while reaching for a hand hold on a rail.

'I thought so, it seems one direction is just as good as another, unless you still want to see France of course?' grinned the maniac to who I had foolishly given over the helm.

'No that's okay, we'll go this way.' I agreed, not wishing to upset Captain Bligh at the wheel.

His need for speed soon diminished and he throttled back to a more reasonable rate of knots. I was relieved as although the fuel tank was quite large, the fuel inside would not last long if we continued to scream about the waves like boy racers in a supermarket car park. The sky that day was clear and bright and the sea rippled softly in small swells. It was a perfect day for Mon Bateau to undergo its sea trials. Sounds very grand - sea trials, but that was exactly what we were doing. We cruised back and forth, and here and there going nowhere but heading somewhere. I had brought my charts with me so while John stood at the helm; I practiced some compass readings and plotting. Of course I knew where we were, I could clearly see land and the harbour but I thought this was an opportunity not to be missed. John's navigation skills were better than mine so he understood my reasoning, best to practice on a bright calm day rather than wait for a blanket of mist to descend or a tempest of biblical proportions to turn the world black and furious.

The day had been perfect and we both wore happy smiles when the time came to head back into the river. Passing through the small harbour presented no problems, however I admit I was feeling somewhat anxious about returning to the hamlet where I moored Mon Bateau. Sure enough I found a welcoming committee waiting for me when I returned to shore. I noticed many had nipped home for a change of clothes but some still showed evidence of that mornings drenching as they encircled me with angry faces. Threats of all kinds were thrown at me while I cringed under the attack, threats to my life, my boat but more importantly, to my manhood rained down on me. John snuck off quietly denying all knowledge of me or my vessel. Finally I managed to calm the storm by professing my lack of intelligence and blaming the whole misadventure on my inexperience in handling the new boat. Some of the still angry crowd continued in their demands that I be hung from the nearest tree but luckily for me, the majority began to accept my pleas for forgiveness and the general mood finally calmed down. Now it was time to open my wallet in the nearby pub, a small price for my mistake. However I had not considered just how much an angry crowd could drink. I went home that evening with an empty wallet, somewhat double vision and an empty stomach. Just the right conditions in which to face an even angrier wife, a tad annoyed that I was drunk, late for my evening meal which was of course ruined, but even more furious at my empty wallet!

I kept the Mon Bateau for several years and used it as often as I could, though often without the company of James. He now had other interests to keep him amused, along with his studies of course. He did accompany me a few times with some of his friends and those days were always enjoyable. James was keen on water sports so it was not long before he convinced me to take him water skiing, or actually it was more of rubber ringing. That is to say I towed a huge rubber ring about the water with him and his friends attempting to stay in it. The ring resembles a car tyre inner tube but costs substantially more, guess who would have to purchase it? Not me that was for sure. I simply scrounged an old tractor sized inner tube, fixed a few holes, cleaned it and told everyone it was the genuine article and cost me a fortune. Sometimes one has to invent ones own kudos! Anyway the Mon Bateau was certainly powerful enough to pull it over the water at huge speeds. I gather the aim of the game was the first one to fall off had to buy the drinks. However staying on it at all was a task too far and by the end of the day, all participates owed me several drinks. I was the only one not to fall off the damn thing. Of course it helped that I was also the only one not to attempt such a feat anyway, I stayed on the boat.

A friend of James did own a pair of water skis and these too were put to use that year. Again I chose to remain dry, able to breath air and at absolutely no risk by staying on board in charge of the Mon Bateau. The boys however had a great time; I would like someone to explain to me how one can enjoy being forcefully ejected from a rubber donut followed by crashing down hard into the cold sea. Please explain the thrill of being somersaulted head over heels before landing face first in the water with ones water skis flying off in all directions. I admit I was too scared to attempt such adrenaline rich activities, but maybe, just maybe I was a little jealous of the youthful health and vitality racing across the water behind me, or flying through the air and still considering hitting the water hard as fun.

Fishing was another activity where James joined me but these trips did not last, neither of us could catch anything and it soon became apparent that our fishing trips often resembled a case of the blind leading the blind. So I began taking others out fishing. I did not often participate but I was happy for the excuse to take Mon Bateau out for a few hours. The Mon Bateau had a spacious cockpit ideal for fishing and the Volvo Penta could potter along at a slow pace as well as thunder across the water. I kept the numbers down to four or less including me when on fishing trips, a hook or two in one's ears quickly decided the numbers. Having too many on board a boat with fishing rods flashing about was certainly hazardous to one's health, especially mine. With my health and safety firmly in mind, I mostly took only one or two people fishing. At one time I even allowed one of my daughter's boyfriends to accompany me out to sea. I had to promise faithfully that I would not throw him over board, accidently or otherwise, before my daughter would allow such a trip but I kept my fingers crossed behind my back whilst making the promise. Everyone knows a promise is void if ones fingers are crossed when making the pledge - don't they?

One grey and overcast day, the boyfriend of the moment joined me on Mon Bateau for a days sea fishing. I had a couple of rods and a box full of lethal and loose hooks, lures, floats and other paraphernalia that one acquired when fishing so I was equipped at least. The boyfriend turned up with enough fishing gear to catch Moby Dick. Off we sailed into the sunset, or grey skies and moody sea in truth. I admit I was not really looking forward to the day, this particular boyfriend made drying paint appealing. But as any good father I gritted my teeth and soldiered on. As we motored down river to the harbour I noticed with some annoyance that the boyfriend had made himself comfortable and was obviously intending to do nothing until the time came to fish. Now most of the folks I had taken on board before all had the good grace to do odd jobs around the boat as a small thank you for the trip. The boyfriend did not appear to be that way inclined, though I admit I was never sure which way he was actually inclined if you get my meaning. Grabbing a bucket and a cloth, I pointed at all the Seagull splatters and politely suggested he do some cleaning, the journey out to sea would take at least half an hour and as I was controlling the boat, it seemed only fair to me that he contributed to the trip.

After several gestures the boyfriend still just sat and looked at me as if I had lost my mind. So making sure my course was safe and I was not going to collide with any stray smugglers or irate customs men, I turned to him and shouted that he get cleaning. His next words shocked me and that takes some doing. He firmly folded his arms and announced that he was not going to clean up any seagull poo, cleaning was women's work. Well to say I was flabbergasted would be an understatement indeed and I very nearly broke the promise to my daughter there and then. Being a lazy bugger on my boat was one thing, but being a chauvinist and my daughter's boyfriend was too much. Jerking the gear lever into neutral I stormed to the rear of the boat and forcefully hauled him to his feet. I then picked up the bucket and cloth and made myself quite clear that it was either cleaning the boat or swimming home, his choice! He chose the bucket and began clearing the poop from my decks. I must admit that deep down I was disappointed, the urge to push him overboard was almost overpowering at that moment.

By the time we reached open water, the boat was clean and we both let that minor episode drop and spoke no more about it. I did resolve to do my utmost to ensure this particular sad excuse for a man did not ever marry my daughter. But it was time to fish so we set about getting our gear ready and preparing the frozen sand eels for the hooks. I did not like using live bait for two reasons. I did not like the idea of shoving a nasty hook through the body of any living creature, and in truth I was too lazy to go and dig out the bait for myself. Instead I purchased it already caught and frozen from a local fishing tackle shop for a matter of pence, by far the better choice for me. I owned two rods plus I had the rod that belonged to James with me. His rod was far better than mine but it was really a casting rod, or so I was told. I had no idea what difference there was, a rod was a rod. I did understand that fishing from a boat was somewhat different to fishing from the shore. One does not need to cast out the line into deeper water, after all one is sat on top of deep water when fishing from a boat. So normally a less flexible and often shorter rod is used, again so I was told. I chose my shortest rod, a rod so inflexible He-Man could not have bent it, but it was the easiest to assemble and I really had no aspirations that I would catch anything. This boat rod could be leaned against the side of the boat while I sipped tea or beer, depending on what was available. I considered there was not the slightest risk of a fish disturbing my rest.

With the bait loaded, we flicked the lines over board and began the wait. I put the engine on tick over which gave me just enough forward motion to steer. Once I considered we were far away enough from any rocks or other vessels entering or exiting the harbour, I turned the engine off and was immediately covered in a blanket of silence as the boat gently drifted on the water. It did not last long however, it quickly became apparent that the boyfriend was a talker. For the next hour or so I had to contend with meaningless waffle about his previous fishing excursions, his job and his ambitions for the future. The thought of throwing him overboard resurfaced in my mind.

The day progressed as we attempted to pit our superior human intelligence against the denizens of the deep, however as we had not caught anything, I decided the fish were winning this battle. Occasionally I had restarted the engine and slowly moved on to another site, hoping that the fish were less intellectual in that area, but to no avail. Both the boyfriend and I had brought a packed lunch for the day, I could make tea or coffee on the gas cooker in the galley but I was not about to attempt a hot meal. Gas, hot food and fluids along with an accident prone chef would be a recipe for disaster on a boat. Of course the boyfriend could not cook, that was women's work he said so it was down to cold sandwiches and chocolate biscuits. How his mother must love him. I wondered how much he weighed, how difficult would it be to feed him to the fish he was trying to catch. I kept my thoughts to myself and restrained myself as any good father does, but plotting his demise entertained me throughout that day.

By now I was becoming bored, bored with dangling a line overboard for fish to laugh at, bored of his endless nattering and bored with just drifting about on the water. Thinking it was a good time to give up and head home, I reached for my rod just as it began to vibrate. Blimey I thought; please do not tell me I have actually caught something. Carefully I raised the rod and began to slowly reel in whatever it was that had found my frozen sand eel attractive. My activity drew the attention of June's boyfriend and within moments he was by my side giving instructions on how I should reel in my catch. It is strange how fishermen and anglers always assume their way is best and that they are expert catchers of fish, even though they themselves had not caught so much as a strand of seaweed. Anyway I continued to reel in slowly, ignoring the words of advice piercing my ears. Slowly, oh so slowly I eased in the line, all the time wondering what would be on the end. A wellington boot perhaps, or a supermarket trolley, they seem to get every where. I certainly did not expect a real live fish. Suddenly a head broke the surface of the water, a fish head! I nearly dropped the rod overboard in surprise when the wriggling body left the water as my line pulled it onboard.

I had caught a fish! Wonder of wonders I thought, what would be next in my extraordinary run of luck. Quickly I landed the fish on the cockpit deck as the boyfriend who nearly wet himself in excitement. Before I could gather my senses and move, he had the fish in his hands and was removing the hook from its mouth. I wondered if he was going to eat it there and then judging from his eagerness. Once the hook was out he showed me what I had caught. It was the ugliest fish I had ever seen! I had no idea what it was, I was only familiar with mackerel and this beastie was totally alien to me. The thing had a large almost square head and was a shade of red in colour. Huge yellow and black eyes stared at me as only fish eyes can do, while three tendrils of some form wiggled on each side of the strange head. I had no clue what it was and I was about to suggest he throw it back in before its mother came looking for us with revenge on her mind.

'It's a Gurnard!' exclaimed the boyfriend in delight.

'What's a Gurnard?' I asked while still staring at the weird creature squirming in his hands.

'It's a Red Gurnard. They are mainly bottom dwellers so this one must have come up far enough to find your bait. They are really good eating, are you going to take it home for tea?'

'Not flaming likely! It's the ugliest thing I've ever seen! Why the heck would I want to eat it?' I enquired incredulously.

'No, no; they're great. You're lucky to have caught one. I've never caught any before. I know they are found off this coast but it's the first I've actually had in my hands. You sure you don't want to take it home to your wife?'

'Er, no I'm fine,' I muttered in horror at the very idea of carrying that thing home and as for what my wife would say if I dropped that thing on her table is unimaginable. 'Why not put it back in the water? After all one fish will hardly make a meal, even if one is brave enough to eat it.'

Alas by now the poor thing had expired so putting it back would not help it one little bit, not that there was any chance of the boyfriend relinquishing the beastie.

'You've got to be joking! If you don't want it, I'll have it. Mum will cook it for me and like I said, they're supposed to taste great. I'll have it for my tea.' With that he wrapped it in his discarded sandwich paper and shoved it deep into his bag. Lovely I thought, a lunch bag stinking of fish. How appetising! Best of luck to him, maybe he will choke of one of it spiny fins. There was always a bright side to my day.

Chapter Seventeen: End of an Era.

I never took the boyfriend fishing again, he did not last long in my daughters affections happily. I did still take many others, but not any of her boyfriends anymore. Instead I ventured out with my friends, a few acquaintances and even the odd enemy or two. I simply enjoyed any excuse to get out on the water and if that meant I had to ferry fishy people around the waves, then so be it. Sometimes I surprised myself by catching something but in the main I caught very little, much to the continuing amusement of my angling companions. I seldom towed skiers or flocks of lazy penguins any more. James and his friends had soon tired of being thrown from a rubber ring or falling off water skis, plus education and partying tended to get in the way. Sadly both my children were growing up and were no longer interested in spending time on my boat with their old dad. My son was in college and my daughter was working for a big firm, though to be fair, my daughter never did really like boats anyway. I too was finding an infuriating interruption to my water activities, that bane of all hobbyists, leisure seekers and law judges – work! I was now so busy I had little time to spend messing about on the river and my boat was returning to its original shade of green through lack of use and maintenance. Luckily I did have a few more adventures on Mon Bateau before I ran out of free time completely and became a total slave to work.

On one such adventure I was asked if I would take a female friend of mine and her family of one husband and two young girls out for a boat trip. Any excuse was good to me so I happily consented. It was simply to be a pleasure trip, down the river and briefly out to sea to see what we could see on the sea. My friend's father used to be a keen boater and she hoped that a trip out on the water would rekindle memories of her late parents. Her husband had no such reasons other than his life's motto of, "*if it's free than take it, no matter what it is or was or will be.*" My friend who I shall name Olivia had two girls, both entering their early teens so a day out with the parents had not yet become boring and socially taboo. The allotted day arrived and luckily, and most unusual for a British summer, the sun was shining and the sky was clear as I made my way down to the river. I took the little tender out to Mon Bateau and quickly got it ready for use, before rowing back to the small slipway before the family arrived. I knew Olivia had experience of boats but I was not sure about her husband and children. Many people turn up for a boat trip dressed in the most inappropriate manner, including the stiletto heels and fancy wide brimmed hats I have already mentioned. Of course I did not expect Olivia's husband to arrive dressed as such, but one never knows.

However when they arrived I was pleased to see that all were suitably attired, though Olivia's choice of clothing caused some disconcertment for a moment or two, before the task of getting them aboard and the boat under way wiped the matter from my mind. The husband Dylan, was dressed as always in old jeans and a t-shirt, the two girls were in shorts and t-shirts suitable for their age, though one was dressed in such a shocking pink, any rescue vessels would have seen us miles away. I hoped that situation would not arise. Olivia received quite a few glances from the old boatmen standing around the tiny quay, chatting as always about their craft and the assorted subjects that old men tend to discuss when gathered in a group. Now it must be said but with absolutely no offence intended that Olivia had a plain sort of appearance, she did not have fashion model looks, but she could still command attention. She was quite tall, slim and with long legs, especial dressed as she was that day. Olivia was a wife and mother and not prone to wearing skimpy clothes. Today was her day though and she made sure men noticed her. In truth it was the shortness of her cut off denim jeans that caught one's attention. The jeans had been cut off quite short and the remaining legs of the garment had been rolled up as far as humanly possible, making her legs appear very long indeed. On her torso she wore only a bikini top, nothing too revealing but taken along with the short cut off jeans, Olivia certainly created some reaction amongst the old men. I had known Olivia a long time so apart from my initial surprise, I gave her attire no more thought. I was too busy to be staring at a pair of legs. Her husband did not appear to mind the furtive glances she was receiving from the old boatmen, confident in the close marriage they shared.

I loaded them all into the tender, making sure the two young girls understood the dangers of the water and instructed them to remain seated and holding on. Dylan fussed about where he would sit but following a meaningful glare from his wife, he duly positioned himself near the girls and became still. Olivia followed last, her experience of boats coming to the fore as she first made sure her family were seated and safe before climbing aboard herself. With the family all on board and their combined weight distributed about the small boat evenly, I pushed off from the quay and once again rowed the tender out to Mon Bateau. By now my arms were beginning to feel the strain but I manfully rowed on, battling the water like a true Viking. Actually I felt more like an orang-utan than a Viking, I swear the oars had stretched my arms.

The trip across the river in my little tender was thankfully uneventful and we reached the Mon Bateau without a major or minor catastrophe. I think the family had expected a small, tried and dilapidated vessel, as I had known them for a long time and more importantly, they had known me. I was not sure if I should have been offended or surprised that they would associate me with a boat wreck, but in truth, even I would associate myself with a boat wreck! Nevertheless I was pleased at their reaction when they caught their first sight of my Mon Bateau gleaming in the sun.

Getting them all aboard the larger vessel, I freed us from the mooring and headed off down river, hoping to give them all a day out they would enjoy. Glancing about the boat, Dylan appeared a little nervous.

Turning to me he asked, 'Do boats like this sink very often?'

'No, usually it's only once,' I replied.

Strangely my answer to his question did not appear adequate and the father of two deemed not to seek any further sage advice from me. Dylan showed little interest in the boat after a brief tour. He seemed content to stare out at the landscape passing by, pointing out birds and any items of interest to his two children. Olivia chatted happily to who ever would listen and it was obvious she was reliving happy memories from her past. When we had passed all the other moored craft, Olivia asked if she could take the helm. I agreed and moved aside so she could grasp the wheel. I had little fear of anything going awry as we were still in the river. I informed her I would take control once again when we entered the harbour. It was not that I did not trust her; she appeared very confident and competent in her handling of my boat. But motoring through the busy harbour was an experience not to be forced on anyone. Even after many years of sailing on the river and passing through the harbour, I still felt nervous on occasion. It was not the amount of traffic one was likely to encounter; it was the stupidity of those one may bump into along the way.

I had become expert at dodging those tiny craft that skip over the water at the command of an inexperienced maritime moron. One also had to contend with the odd sailor who insisted on the right of way on the water, engine power must always give way to sail power. Now this rule is fine if correctly adhered to, but some stick to the rule in its extreme. It is utter absurdity to try and force a thousand ton vessel to move aside for a half ton sailing yacht. However several have been known to foolishly attempt this. A story from years back came to my mind.

An inexperienced but arrogant sailor leaving the harbour one day encountered a huge cargo vessel heading straight for him as it entered the harbour. With the rule on his mind, the sailor refused to move out of the way and held his course. The cargo vessel also continued on its course because it had no choice. A true David and Goliath scenario unfolded within the peaceful waters of the harbour. Locals put down their beers and holiday makers forgot their cameras as each and every onlooker eagerly awaited the outcome. Stray dogs stopped sniffing, cat stopped prowling and the local policeman actually paused in his consumption of a doughnut. The harbour watched and waited. It takes a vast area of water for a large vessel to turn and it also requires a great distance to halt its forward motion. A small yacht can turn on a sixpence as the saying goes, unlike a massive ship with a heavy cargo, and can stop quite quickly. Another other factor in this uneven battle is that the wheel house on the cargo ship is high above the water. The yacht skipper can certainly see the tower block of a ship chugging towards him, but the captain high above the water in the control bridge on a ship of floating steel may not be able to see a small plastic craft low on the water.

I was not there that day but witnesses have retold the story in pubs far and wide about what happened that day. From the stories told, the yacht skipper eventually realised the cargo ship was not going to abide by the rule of sail before engine but by then it was too late. Witnesses retell the skipper's frantic efforts to get his pride and joy out of the way of the steel monster bearing down on him. With his white shorts rapidly turning brown, the yacht skipper began adjusting his sails in frenzy. He even starting his onboard engine in a desperate attempt to get out of the way, shouting furiously at the other people on his boat. Typically they ignored his despairing pleas, confident that these things only happened to others on television, it could not possibly happen to them. Alas it did, the skipper managed to get out of the way of the sharp bow heading straight at his boat, but not far enough. The cargo vessel's forward side of the bow caught the stern of the little yacht, ripping it off as easy as a knife through hydrogenated fat spread. Luckily enough local craft had witnessed the accident and were able get the passengers and the now not so arrogant skipper off the yacht before it sank. No one was hurt but the skipper's pride suffered a bigger blow than his boat had sustained. His day failed to improve when he received a hefty fine from the harbour authorities for his utter lack of boatmanship.

So with this and many other stories in mind, I elected to take charge of our route through the harbour. I was pleased to note Olivia made no objections, she obviously realised the possible dangers. Once out at sea

I allowed her to take charge again, her husband still showed no inclination to try his hand at steering the boat and I was certainly not suicidal enough to offer the wheel to either of the young girls. While Olivia steered the Mon Bateau, I remained seated at the stern and waved at all my friends and acquaintances we passed as we headed further out to sea. I admit I was enjoying the looks of astonishment on their faces as they realised I had a scantily clad woman at the helm. No doubt the gossip would reverberate around the pub that night! I did not mind at all, I could already feel my ego rising and my `street credibility' rating soaring high above its normal non-existent level. Once far enough out, I instructed Olivia to turn to starboard so we could sail along the coast and allow her husband and children to see the shore line from the sea. They knew many of the locations we passed and their delighted chatter and laughter drifted back to me as I semi-slumbered on the stern seat.

The time came for refreshments and I offered to make cups of tea and coffee for my guests. Dylan was sat at the bow, getting constantly drenched by the wave spray arching up over the bow. I considered him stupid until I realised a play between man and wife was in progress. Olivia was deliberately heading into the large waves at speed, knowing Dylan would get wet. Dylan on the other hand, knew exactly what his wife was up to and refused to acknowledge his discomfort, instead he put on a brave face and pretended to be enjoying the experience. The two girls were lying on the cabin roof, each following my instructions and holding on firmly to a hand rail as they too appeared to be enjoying themselves. Though it was my boat and theoretically I was in charge, I chose not to comment on Olivia's driving or her husbands soaking figure. I deemed it wise to stay out of marital exchanges.

Making my way to the companion way, I entered the cabin and fired up the small gas cooker. I had remembered to bring a plastic container full of fresh water and now I used this to fill my whistle kettle. While that boiled I prepared a tea for me and coffees for Olivia and Dylan, Olivia having bought soft drinks for her two girls. I opened a packet of biscuits I had also packed for the trip and then made the drinks. Now for those who know, most pleasure boats affordable to the average boater have a small and cramped cabin. Most have only enough room for two bunks, a cooker and a sink. The Mon Bateau was slightly larger and contained a toilet as well, posh huh? Anyway the entrance in and out of the cabin was through a miniscule passage that separated the galley from the heads. The gap between the two departments was so small one could turn the kettle on while doing what is necessary on the toilet. I hasten to add I was not attempting this form of dexterity on that day.

The coffee and tea made, I picked up two mugs of steaming beverage and turned to make my way out from the cabin. The low ceiling caused me to hunch over with my head down, so I could not actually see where I was going but as it was only a couple of steps, I saw no reason for full visibility. Suddenly my forward motion came to an abrupt halt and I found my startled face jammed firmly between Olivia's thighs! Without me noticing, she had shifted her position at the helm slightly to the left, obviously trying to make herself more comfortable as she stood steering the boat. Now she was standing right across the cabin doorway, her legs apart for stability and her attention fully on controlling the boat and soaking her husband. Her attention soon moved to the confused head stuck firmly between her long legs.

For several moments I could not understand what was obstructing me, to be honest I was struggling to ensure I did not spill any of the hot coffee on my sandaled feet. It took my bewildered brain a few seconds to realise my face was pressed up against female flesh. And then another few . . . several seconds for me to decide whether to remove it or not. However decency demanded I retreat so with a muttered apology I withdrew my now red face from that intimate area and moved a pace backwards. I actually expected Dylan to rush over and thump me on the nose for my unintentional actions, but a glance through the forward cabin window showed he was still staring out to sea. Luckily for me perhaps, he had not noticed anything untoward going on behind him. The two girls were out of sight on the cabin roof so the little episode was known only to me and Olivia. I waited for a scream of indignation from Olivia, but to my surprise she simply stepped half a pace backwards before looking down at me with a small smile on her face. I could do nothing but apologise when she finally stepped to one side and allowed me to exit the cabin. Silently and with a quick glance to where her husband still sat, she indicated that I should not attract the attention of the others. Without another word, Olivia returned to her position at the helm and away from the cabin doorway. I handed her the coffee and made sure the redness of my face had subsided before calling to Dylan that his coffee was ready.

The experience of finding ones face between the thighs of a married woman on board boat is not one I would have expected, however I will admit it was a bonus. I was very embarrassed but Olivia appeared to give my mishap no more thought, it was as if the incident never happened. Nonetheless I found it very difficult to look Dylan straight in the eye for several weeks. As far as I know, he remains in the dark as to my head being between his wife's thighs and I am certainly not going to mention it.

Another odd couple accompanied me out on the boat one day when my resistance was down and I was open to foolish gestures. The couple were what in today's world is often classed as middle aged, however to me they were both knocking on a bit and I may have considered them a tad older than middle aged. I knew the gent through an acquaintance and the woman as a close acquaintance of the gent, very close if you get my meaning. The gent was called Aubrey and was in his sixties at least, tall and thin with grey hair. He was known to view the world through rose coloured glasses, a trait that can quickly become annoying. His lady friend was called Betty, shorter than Aubrey and certainly wider than Aubrey and then some! She had long auburn hair, obviously dyed and way too much lipstick. However Betty and Aubrey made a very nice couple, friendly and well meaning. So how could I refuse Betty's request for a boat trip? I refer to them both as a couple because that is what they were. Marriage was on Betty's to do list, along with other mundane items such as holidays and a new house, but unfortunately it was not on Aubrey's list. It was not that he did not want to marry Betty, it was more the case of he simply could not be bothered. They already lived together and shared all the pleasures a married couple share, like arguments. So why spend money on a piece of paper to get what he already had, anyway Aubrey hated making plans or decisions of any kind so he was happy where he was.

The day arrived and I met Betty and Aubrey down on the slipway. I was pleased to see Betty had dressed accordingly, I was sure she would turn up in her normal high heels and skirt but instead she wore flat shoes and jeans. Aubrey turned up looking his usual self, a walking scarecrow. Getting them on the dinghy surprised me. I was expecting Betty to be nervous and hesitant but I was wrong, it was Aubrey who provided the problems and the entertainment for the day. Again it was the female member of the couple who admitted to having experience of boats. What is it with the women I knew, did they all hang around boats and sailors in their youth? A bit dodgy I thought but wisely kept my thoughts to myself. Sadly in complete opposition it quickly became apparent that the only experience Aubrey had of boats and water activities were from his television or his bath. Getting him to understand that a boat will move when one gets into it, and the fact that one must hold on to something at all times was a task almost too far for that average human being to contemplate.

Eventually I managed to get Aubrey aboard without him getting wet, though it did come close. He chose to ignore the warnings from both Betty and me when climbing down into the dinghy. With one foot still on the slipway and one foot in the boat, Aubrey took no account of the fact that the boat would move.

Suddenly he found himself straddling a space of water with nowhere to go. The boat had moved away from the slipway as soon as he put his foot in it. Aubrey obviously kept his weight completely central as his legs widened alarmingly. My instructions concerning weight distribution had evidently passed from one ear to the next without stopping. I had explained that when boarding a small and irrationally mobile boat, one should move smoothly from shore to boat, shifting one's weight from land to boat without hesitation. This way, one's centre of gravity is either on land or in the vessel, having one's weight hovering above the water is definitely not a good idea! It was only the quick thinking and reaction of Betty that saved him from falling into the water between the boat and the slipway, or splitting himself in two. Not an action recommended for any age group. With one forceful tug, Betty grabbed one flailing arm and pulled him into the boat where he landed in a jumble of limbs. Once untangled and safely aboard in the small tender, Aubrey continued to demonstrate a total lack of understanding concerning the physics of moving about on a boat. He failed to comprehend that attempting to stand on one side of the boat would cause the boat to tip; again it was Betty that shouted at him to sit down and keep still.

Assured that Betty would keep control of the nautical disaster known as Aubrey, I turned to the ring attached to the slipway that enabled boats to tie up alongside it. I untied my bow line and . . . .

Suddenly I realised the tender had begun to spin! It began spinning in a circle on the water upon the instant I released the line. I was nearly catapulted overboard as I scrabbled to find my balance in the whirling boat. I quickly glanced about me, expecting the movement to be caused by the wake of a passing boat or even a mysterious whirlpool. I even wondered if my small boat had fallen into the grasp of a water born poltergeist, what other explanation could there be? Then I heard Betty's voice and turned to discover what she was shouting about. The answer I sought became apparent instantly. It was not a wake or a whirlpool, and it was clearly not a poltergeist. It was Aubrey!

Aubrey was rowing furiously, puffing and panting in his efforts to move the small craft across the water. A look of pure concentration lined his face as he bent his back and put all his strength into his actions. But all his efforts failed spectacularly as Aubrey again

348

demonstrated his complete lack of nautical understanding or even common sense. Aubrey was trying to row my boat with only one oar! Not both oars as one would expect, but just one. He had hold of the oar on his side of the boat and was pulling with all his might. No wonder the boat was spinning, the daft bugger appeared oblivious to the requirement of two oars to propel this form of vessel forward, or even backwards on the water. Struggling to maintain my balance, I reached over and quickly removed the oar from his uncomprehending grasp, ordering him sternly to move back and sit down beside a furious Betty. Once I was sure Betty had a firm strangle hold on Aubrey, I grasped both oars and began rowing, in the correct manner, out to Mon Bateau and pondering on what I had let myself in for.

The entertainment resumed once more when we arrived alongside the Mon Bateau. Before we could stop him, Aubrey had leapt to his feet and attempted to scramble on board the bigger boat. Again he failed to understand that water moves, and anything on the water moves. From his position on the opposite side of the tender, Aubrey attempted to reach across Betty and grab hold of Mon Bateau's hand rail. Of course the tender moved backwards and away from the other boat, opening a gap between both vessels. Aubrey never reached the hand rail but his forward motion coupled with the backward movement of the tender came close to seeing him dive head first in the water. Instead he landed in an untidy heap on Betty's unsuspecting lap, an action that failed to amuse his partner. With an expression of exasperation, Betty's hand shot out like a snake strike and caught hold of Aubrey's shirt tail.

'Sit down you damn fool!' she shouted angrily, 'You're a damn menace and don't know a thing about boats, so stop trying to be helpful and keep still. We'll tell you want to do when it needs to be done. Shut up and sit down!'

Betty had pulled Aubrey back upright and forcefully swung him back onto the seat. I felt a pang of sorrow for Aubrey when I witnessed the vigour with which Betty slammed him down on the seat. However my sorrow did not last long, replaced by one of pleasure at his pain, and I was happy to see his pain reflected the pain he was giving us, a pain in the arse!

As was my custom, I had rowed out to the Mon Bateau before Betty and Aubrey arrived and made it ready to sail so there was nothing Aubrey could harm, least that is what I hoped. Once they were safely aboard, I instructed Aubrey to sit still and wait while I cast off the mooring line and started the engine. Without thinking clearly, I passed the mooring line back to Aubrey and innocently asked him to store it away. I thought giving him something to do would lift his spirits and make him feel useful. Climbing back from the bow, I stood at the helm and pushed the throttle forward to get us moving. Slowly I motored through the collection of other vessels that were moored around me, and headed down river towards the harbour. All went well and the couple sat peacefully admiring the scenery along the river side as I steered us though the harbour and out onto the sea. The day remained bright and I was beginning to relax, happy to show off my boat's abilities and ensure Betty and Aubrey enjoyed themselves on their day out.

We had sailed about a mile out from the harbour mouth when I asked if either of them would like a spot of mackerel fishing. Both replied that they would and Betty commented on previous fishing trips with her parents. Aubrey of course had no experience of fishing, other than carrying fish home along with some chips and wrapped in paper. On board I had a couple of mackerel lines with spinning lures attached, so the need for bait did not arise - thankfully. I put the engine in neutral and turned to get the fishing equipment, and promptly fell flat on my face. I had tripped on an untidy heap of rope that some fool had left lying on the cockpit floor. I knew instantly who the fool was. Aubrey had not stored the mooring line; he had simply bundled it up and thrown it on the cockpit floor. Swearing quietly I picked myself up and began sorting out the rope. With stern words, I pointed out to Aubrey that one does not just dump rope on the deck because some poor klutz may fall over it, just like I had. It was my fault I know, I should not have entrusted the task to someone as nautically inept as Aubrey. But we live and learn - if we are lucky enough with Aubrey around. Once the rope was coiled and stored I retrieved the mackerel lines and handed Betty and Aubrey one each. We had all brought a packed lunch and flasks of tea so when I had supplied them both with fishing lines and ensured the lines were a suitable distance from the propeller, we all sat down with a hot drink and awaited the mackerel.

Suddenly Aubrey twitched, that is to say he jumped up from his seat and with a mighty heave he pulled in his line. Frantically Aubrey wound in his line with a fierce look upon his face, the look of a hunter catching his prey. Of course there was nothing attached to the hook at the end of the line. Betty immediately demanded to know what the heck he was playing at; she had almost spilt her tea on her lap when he leapt up.

'I though I'd caught a fish. I felt something on the line so I pulled it in,' was his lame explanation.

'The line has only just gone in the water! You've got to give it time, most fish are not suicidal and don't race to get themselves caught. Now sit down and drink your tea,' admonished Betty with a growl.

'But I felt something . .'

'I don't care what you felt. You've never fished before as far as I know, so how can you tell if you've caught a fish?' demand Betty.

It quickly became apparent that Aubrey did not in fact, have a single clue about fishing. Despite his age, he had never fished nor had he ever been on a small boat. So with great patience, Betty began explaining to him what to expect when a fish caught his line, how to hold the mackerel line and the apparatus it was attached to. Sorry but I do not know what the thingy is called. My best description would be two parallel plastic bars joined together by cross pieces that the line wound around. A simple device that did not require much intelligence, however Aubrey appeared mystified by the gadget. Betty showed Aubrey how to hold the line very gently between his fingers, allowing it to move with the water currents and assured him he would feel a series of gently tugs on the line when he had caught a fish. Unfortunately a gentle grip was totally alien to Aubrey. In fact I could see his knuckles were white with the strength of which he held onto the thin fishing line.

Moments after Betty giving futile lessons in fishing to Aubrey she let out a soft cry. With patience and a steady hand, Betty reeled in the first fish of the day. I had a bucket ready and with a practiced hand she removed the hook and placed the wriggling mackerel into the bucket. Aubrey was astounded. I do not think he had ever seen a live fish before judging by his reaction. Immediately he reached into the bucket and grasped the fish for a closer inspection. The inevitable followed. Aubrey lifted the silver mackerel up to his face for a closer look, the fish, as all fish do, wriggled furiously in his hand and with a shout of surprise, Aubrey loosened his grasp. Free from the fumbling human hand, the fish flew from his grip and went straight over the side and back into the water. To say Betty was mad would be an understatement, her voice rose and her choice of words surprised even me as she shouted her frustration at the dumbfounded Aubrey. To be honest, I was absolutely flabbergasted at his stupidity and childlike inability to use common sense; however Betty was saying everything I was thinking so I kept quiet.

For the next hour or so, Betty pulled in several fish and placed them in the bucket, well away from Aubrey's reach. Poor Aubrey did not catch a single thing; if he had I am sure he would have pulled its head off in his desperation to get it on board. The art of playing a fish on the line was not a concept Aubrey could relate to. I could emphasise with him that day, after all, I was certainly not the greatest fisherman. I was not the worst, because one has to first catch a fish to be considered good or bad at the sport to obtain a rating at it. I had not yet acquired any form of rating in the noble art of fishing. What ever my rating on the skills ladder of fishermen, I firmly believed I stood far above Aubrey.

With enough fish caught for a decent meal, Betty decided that was enough fishing for the day and asked if she could take a turn at the helm. I was quite happy to relinquish the wheel as it was time for a cuppa. I was sure Betty could handle the boat so I instructed her in what course to follow, pointing out the bearing on my gimbal compass. A heading was not really necessary as we were out in clear water, but it gave her a sense of direction. We all munched on our lunches while Betty competently steered the boat which motored along at a sedate pace whilst we gazed at the scenery and other craft in the vicinity. By now Aubrey had begun to fidget again, he was becoming bored and I could tell by his actions that he needed to be doing something. However what does one suggest to an accident prone, clumsy and nautical inexperience individual? After some thought, I concluded that I would let him steer the Mon Bateau back to the harbour while Betty sat and had her lunch. Aubrey of course had eaten his lunch in almost one bite, gobbling down the food as if tomorrow or even the next five minutes would never come. What harm could come of him simply steering the boat?

I instructed Aubrey to head for the mouth of the harbour, nothing too demanding I thought. Once he was settled behind the wheel, I went and sat beside Betty, content in the knowledge that even Aubrey could not come to any harm just taking the boat back home. I was wrong. Betty and I chatted amiably about the local coastline and any items of interest. She related stories of her childhood on her father's boat and compared the boats of yesteryear to those gleaming plastic vessels of today. I admit I was foolishly not taking much notice of what Aubrey was doing as my attention was on what Betty was saying. We were discussing the shoreline and how it had changed over the years when I absentmindedly noticed the shoreline and the towering rocks ominously close. Suddenly realisation dawned! We should not be this close to the rocks. I leapt from my seat and rushed to see what Aubrey was doing.

'What the heck are you doing?' I asked.

'Nothing! I'm steering the boat like you told me to.' was his unconcerned reply.

'But you're heading for the rocks!'

Aubrey peered around and then incredulously asked, 'What rocks?'

'Those great black things there,' I almost shouted while pointing at the geological features in question.

Quickly I took the wheel from his grasp and turned the Mon Bateau sharply, praying that I still had enough distance to make the manoeuvre. I also prayed my squeaking buttocks could not be heard as I strove to avoid a collision. Luckily we did not strike the rocks and I sailed us out into wider water once more. We had been heading for the rocky shoreline to our left or port of the harbour, some distance away from the harbour mouth itself. Once back on course I again instructed Aubrey to steer towards the centre of the harbour mouth. I also gave him a compass bearing in the hope that between the visual sight of the harbour and the compass, he would get it right this time. Satisfied he could not go wrong, I returned to my seat beside Betty. We were still some distance from the harbour so I thought I would have time to continue our chat before I took over the controls.

Again my attention was on Betty as she regaled me with stories from the past. Looking out to port, I could see we were nowhere near the rocks this time so I fully believed Aubrey had come to his senses. But wait, surely the rocks should not be that far away? Twisting my head round I saw that although we were no longer in danger of hitting the shoreline on the left of the harbour, we were in fact heading straight for the other side! Here we go again I thought.

'Aubrey! Where are you going this time?' I called to the witless helmsman.

'I'm still doing what you told me to, I'm heading for the harbour of course!' was his slightly terse reply.

'No you're not!' I shouted as once again I had to leave my seat and take control of the wheel.

'Why are you not steering?' I asked Aubrey.

'But I am! I've not turned the wheel at all. I've kept it in a straight line all the time.'

'But this is a boat! It won't stay in a straight line. It's moved by the sea and tides. You have to actually turn the wheel and physically steer to where you want to go.'

'Oh!' Aubrey muttered after a long pause, 'It works in my car, so why won't the boat stay in a straight line? Is there something wrong with the steering?'

'No there's nothing wrong with the steering, providing you actually steer and don't just stand there hoping the boat will know its own way home!'

I was now past trying to be polite and understanding. Firmly I told him to go and sit down and not touch anything. I stayed at the helm and once again corrected our course. I simply could not understand how someone could be so unable to comprehend the basic knowledge that, unlike a road under the wheels of a car, the sea is constantly moving. A boat must fight against the tides pushing the craft one way, the wind trying to push it another and the general action of waves and currents all striving to undermine the intended direction of a vessel on water. Behind me I could hear Betty berating Aubrey for his thick headedness and stupidity, declaring she would never, ever take him on a boat again. Not without throwing him overboard at least. At that moment I felt sorry for Aubrey. Everything he had do was done with good intentions, from rowing in a circle, to trying to pull the heads off fish, to holding the helms wheel in a firm grasp and ensuring it did not move an inch. Basically Aubrey was not really suited to a nautical life. I also concluded I would not seek his assistance in any DIY jobs, especially when the situation required the use of power tools such as drills or, heaven forbid, an angle grinder!

Alas, Betty and Aubrey were amongst the last guests I took out on Mon Bateau, work was eating away at any spare time I once had. With my son James now fully occupied with his studies, he seldom came out with me on the boat anymore. My wife and daughter remained firm in their disinterest towards anything to do with being on the water and in truth; I too was beginning to grow bored. Not bored of sailing, fishing or other assorted water activities, but bored of doing nothing with Mon Bateau other than cleaning it occasionally and bailing it out frequently. I suppose I could also blame my advancing years but that would not be a realistic excuse. Many of my fellow boat users out aged me by at least a decade, some even stretched to three decades, so age was no reason for giving up. I began to resent having to spend part of my limited free time checking and bailing out the Mon Bateau, though I longed to return to those sunny days on the water. Funny how all our pleasant memories centre round long days of sunshine when in truth, and this being Britain, a sunny day was something of a rarity. So I reluctantly decided to sell my pride and joy, hoping the new owner of Mon Bateau would treasure it as much as I did, and pay a good sum for it of course.

I sold Mon Bateau with a heavy heart but a much thicker wallet. As is always the course of fate and the universe, a couple of months later my work load eased and I found I had time on my hands again. The sun shone and I missed my boat and the life that I enjoyed on the water and all those friends I had come across during my years as a boat user. However on this rare occasion, my heart was over ruled by my head, and my wife. I did buy another boat but a much smaller and simpler craft. I remain to this day, the owner of a thirteen foot long open boat powered by a marvellous electric motor. No more pulling furiously on starter cords, no more mixing fuel and hoping to heck the damn thing would not break down or blow up. No more noise, no more swearing at Seagull engines and no more making repairs on a muddy river bank. Now I bring my small boat home on a trailer at the end of each season and work on it while remaining in easy reach of a warm house and a boiling kettle. With my little boat and the light and easy to handle electric motor, I can spend as many happy hours pottering about on the river as my soul desires. Strangely my wife now seems to enjoy our river trips. She repeated that she never felt safe on a big spacious and powerful vessel, but felt quite safe on a small boat. Yep, strange I know but there it is so who am I too argue, I simply go with the flow so to speak. My daughter now has a family of her own and my son has a partner and his own home so I either go out on my boat alone or on the odd occasion with my wife. However, things could be looking up, I have a young grandson who already loves boats and the water but I may have to wait until he is a little older. But we will see . . . .

FIN

www.ingramcontent.com/pod-product-compliance
Lightning Source LLC
La Vergne TN
LVHW051620080426
835511LV00016B/2094